Glorious Triumphs

Other Books by Vernon Pizer

Revised Edition

VERNON PIZER

Glorious Triumphs

Athletes Who Conquered Adversity

Illustrated with photographs

DODD, MEAD & COMPANY · NEW YORK

1 2 3 4 5 6 7 8 9 10

Library of Congress Cataloging in Publication Data

Pizer, Vernon, date
    Glorious triumphs.

    Includes index.
    SUMMARY: Brief biographies of Barney Ross, Babe
Didrikson, Gordie Howe, Althea Gibson, Glenn Cunningham,
Jerry Kramer, Pete Gray, Tenley Albright, Carol Heiss,
Alonzo Wilkins, Ben Hogan, Paul Berlenbach, Sammy Lee,
and Jim Hurtubise—all athletes who persevered against
great odds to attain prominence in their chosen sport.
    1. Athletes—Biography—Juvenile literature.
[1. Athletes] I. Title.
GV697.A1P5   1980   796'.092'2 [B]   [920]   79-6648
ISBN 0-396-07793-5

For Noah Langdale, Jr., and his "glorious triumphs"—on the gridiron and then as President of Georgia State University

Contents

Introduction

SOMETIMES A BOOK seems to develop a life and a momentum of its own, and when that happens the author has the deep satisfaction of knowing that his words have struck a responsive chord among his readers. That has been the good fortune with this book, which appeared originally in 1968. Readers insisted that it not be permitted to fade away, that it be republished and reissued. This has now been done, but this *Glorious Triumphs* is not merely a reprint of a popular book. It remains faithful to the original version but moves beyond it, expanding its scope. New "glorious triumphs" have been added and old ones have been polished smoother, honed sharper. What remains unchanged is the viewpoint about sports and about the indomitable human spirit.

Sport is a vast panorama painted larger than life. It is infinite in its variety, its moods, its appeal. It is spectacle and color and pageant, thrills and suspense, brute strength, and exquisite finesse. It is movement, speed, endurance, drama, seconds that are split into fragments. It has its own repertoire of sounds—the sharp crack of a bat

9

meeting a ball squarely, the hiss of a waxed ski streaking over close-packed snow, the twang of a tautly strung racket, the roar of the crowd. It has its own smells—the sweat, the wintergreen, the rubbing alcohol, the woodsy scent of tanbark, the faintly fruity, slightly pungent odor of wet leather. Sport has its own language and customs and myths, its halls of fame, its chroniclers, its records and statistics.

But sport is more than its sights and its sounds and its smells, more than the scoreboard and the stopwatch and the record book. More than anything else, sport is people.

This book is about some of those people who have made sport the gripping, fascinating thing that it is. It is not solely an account of their athletic prowess because a superb sports performance should be seen to be appreciated to the full—when it is described it necessarily loses some of its glisten, some of its shimmer, like a hooked trout that has been drawn up on a stream bank. This book tries to capture the quality of the performer even more than the quality of the performance. It is the story behind the exploit rather than simply the exploit itself that is the theme running through the pages that follow.

The athletes who are gathered together in this book are linked by a common bond that extends beyond the playing field or the stadium. They achieved their triumphs in spite of adversity, and their triumphs were the more glorious for that. Each of them encountered handicaps, reverses, obstacles that would have stopped lesser men and women. Each of them, despite the special burden, fought through to the winner's circle. They share a distinctive brand of courage, of persistence, and of faith in themselves, that make their stories more than an entry in a record book.

On April 10, 1899, Theodore Roosevelt, speaking before the Hamilton Club in Chicago, said: "Far better it is to dare mighty things, to win glorious triumphs, even though checkered by failure, than to take rank with those poor spirits who neither enjoy much nor suffer much, because they live in the gray twilight that knows not victory nor defeat."

This book is dedicated to the "Glorious Triumphs" and to those who made them.

—Vernon Pizer

Washington, D.C.

1   The Kid from the Ghetto

Barney Ross

A KNIFE-EDGE WIND cut past the dilapidated tenements in Chicago's ghetto that December morning in 1924. It was only 7:30 but Isadore Rasofsky had already been at work for over an hour in his tiny grocery off Maxwell Street. Nobody knows precisely what happened next. All that is tragically clear is that two armed hoodlums entered the store, shot the shopkeeper, and fled. For two and a half days the spark of life flickered in the grocer's work-worn body, then it burned out.

Isadore Rasofsky was not the sole victim of the senseless, savage slaying. His widow, shocked into an emotional breakdown, had to be sent to out-of-town relatives to try to recover. Because there was no alternative, the three youngest of the five Rasofsky children were placed in an orphanage. The two remaining boys, fourteen and fifteen, were somehow sandwiched into a cousin's already crowded flat.

It was Barney, the fourteen-year-old, who seemed to take the tragedy hardest. He had been especially close to his father and the callous shooting left him with a rage to strike back. He haunted the streets in a fruitless, planless search for the killers until the passion spent itself and he was left with the bitter hurt and the conviction that the only way to beat the ghetto was to beat it into submission.

So Barney became a neighborhood roughneck always in the thick of every street fight. On the face of it, it seemed ludicrous because he was skinny, short, and subject to asthmatic attacks. But he was quick on his feet, dancing around his opponents so that their blows seldom struck him squarely. And every time he lashed out he felt a surge of satisfaction because, in a sense, he was lashing out against his father's slayers.

Barney, the pugnacious neighborhood brawler, was still the old Barney under the newly acquired exterior of toughness, still a boy mourning deeply for the family that had been shattered and wanting desperately to gather together again the remnants that were left. He wanted his mother back, the younger children out of the orphanage, and all of them restored under their own roof. And that required money they did not have. Nor was that his only money problem. His older brother had found a job to help pay their cousin for their board. Barney wanted to pay his own way. Whatever was left over would go into a fund to bring the family together again. So Barney hustled after-school jobs to bring in some money, not a great deal but something. He worked hard because he was sweating his way to a goal that was terribly important to him.

The passing weeks left an imprint on the youngster. His gruelling, self-imposed routine was marking him with a ruggedness, a resiliency he had not possessed earlier. He was still convinced that the key to survival in the ghetto was a cocked fist, but between school and work there was now little time for brawling. Besides, neighborhood toughs were becoming less eager to tangle with him. They were learning that where once Barney had simply been fast on his feet—a weaving, bobbing target whose punches could be shrugged off—now he was becoming a real threat in a fight because muscle had been added to his lean frame.

By the end of the school year Barney's mother had recovered sufficiently to return to Chicago. Barney found a full-time job and he and his brother rented a small, cheap apartment for their mother and themselves. On his regular visits to the orphanage to see the younger children, Barney assured them they would be coming home soon. But whatever money came in seeped right out for food, rent, and doctor's bills; even with both boys working, the Rasofskys could not get ahead of their expenses. Frustration gnawed at Barney; his promises to the younger children had a mocking ring in his ears. Then he discovered a possible way to supplement the family income.

Scattered through fight-happy Chicago were many small gyms staging weekly amateur boxing cards whose winners received gold medals or watches convertible into cash via the nearest pawnshop. That Barney knew nothing of the science of boxing, had never been in a ring or fought with gloves on, did not even register on him. All that registered was the chance to pick up some extra cash to help unlock the orphanage door. He began making the rounds of the grubby, little gyms and after several weeks of trying managed to get a spot on a card.

A more rambunctious, unscientific boxing match than that three-rounder may never have been put on, but the

freewheeling fight pleased the crowd and the referee dip-
lomatically ruled it a draw, awarding gold medals to each
contestant. Barney hocked his the next day for three dol-
lars and was sitting on top of the world. He was back on
the card the following Saturday night. This time he
gained a clear victory. Another medal; another visit to the
pawnshop. From then on Barney was a regular on the
fight circuit, appearing in two or three clubs each week
and winning most of his matches. He was still wildly unscientific, but so were most of his opponents. The difference was that Barney had more speed and more determination than most.

After he turned sixteen, Barney moved up from the
118-pound bantamweights to the 126-pound featherweight class. By now his name was starting to appear occasionally on the sports pages. He had been keeping his
boxing secret from his mother to avoid adding to her
worries; to continue the secret as long as possible he
adopted the ring name of Barney Ross.

Barney was driving himself hard—holding down a full-
time job clerking in a mail-order house and fighting three
or four times a week—and he realized he had to choose
one or the other. Because he figured he might make
more in the ring than in his ill-paying job, he opted for
fighting. After quitting his job he continued leaving home
each morning as though headed for work, going to the
gym instead. A few weeks later his secret life was exposed
when he came home battered from a going-over in the
ring. Mrs. Rasofsky cried and Barney pleaded. It ended
in something like a draw, with Barney granted reluctant
permission to continue fighting until he had earned

enough to bring the children back from the orphanage or until he got hurt, whichever came first.

Barney haunted the gyms, training hard and studying the techniques of the professionals. Occasionally he'd get a chance to spar with one of the pros and some of their ring craft would rub off on him. The old-timers liked Barney—they admired his "moxie"—and they started giving him pointers, things like how to feint and to defend, how to hook and jab, how to strengthen arms and legs and sharpen footwork, how to develop breathing. He was becoming less the freewheeling street fighter, more the skilled boxer. He was now fighting as often as five times a week. In 1928 he won over 200 fights—more than a quarter of them by knockouts—and lost only three. Local fight fans and pawnbrokers were starting to know Barney Ross quite well.

In 1929 Barney decided to enter the Golden Gloves. He knew he'd be up against the best amateurs in the state, each straining for a crack at the Chicago crown and the trip to New York to meet the Golden Gloves champions of that area.

He had his flaws and moments of wildness in his first Golden Gloves bout—still, Barney was good enough to win by a TKO. He looked even better in his next elimination bout, but this time his opponent was also better; Barney took it by a decision. In the finals he was pitted against a fighter who had created a stir in downstate boxing circles and was figured to win. From start to finish it was close. But Barney was faster and that gave him the edge—he was awarded the victory and the Chicago crown. Overnight he had become a ghetto celebrity.

At the intercity showdown in New York the bouts had gone badly for Chicago by the time Barney's turn came. The pressure was on him to strike a blow for Chicago, but from the opening bell he knew he had much more than municipal pride to worry about. In previous encounters, agile footwork and split-second moves had given him an advantage, but this time it was cancelled out by an opponent who could match his speed and agility. It developed into a hard-fought, lightning-fast bout that excited the crowd and at the end of the three-rounder both weary, gasping boxers drew an ovation. The judges rated the fight a draw and ordered a fourth round to break the deadlock. Both men had counted on only three rounds and had put everything they had into each of them. Now they had to find a reserve of strength to carry them through another round. Barney found it, his opponent didn't—is was as simple as that. Barney Ross climbed out of the ring the intercity Golden Gloves featherweight champion.

After returning to Chicago he continued fighting on the amateur cards around town but he began thinking of trying to make it as a pro. He knew the Golden Gloves crown was no guarantee of success in the professional ranks, but he was driven by the need to go after the purses that could get the younger children out of the orphanage. So at the age of eighteen Barney Ross took the plunge into professionalism.

His speedy footwork got him his first break: a place as one of the sparring partners traveling with Jackie Fields, the welterweight titleholder. Fields' manager counted on Barney's speed to help keep the champ sharp.

As a member of the Fields stable, Barney was able to

pick up spots in the preliminary matches and he had a run of luck, winning decisions over a half-dozen no-bodies. In the process, he discovered how rocky was the road that lay ahead. For one thing, he was fighting six-rounders where previously he had only gone three or four rounds; the longer distance strained him to the limit. For another thing, he was now meeting men who were not in it for the transient glory of a medal; this was their full-time, deadly serious business and they were out for blood. Barney was finding out what it was to get butted and thumbed and low-blowed by accomplished practitioners.

After his initial string of pro victories, Barney dropped his eighth bout in a close decision. The loss made him face facts. Being in the Fields stable had served him well as a way to get his feet wet in the pro ranks, but now it could sink him because everything was necessarily geared to the needs of Fields. As a junior member of the en-tourage he couldn't get the kind of managerial attention he had to have to achieve anything worthwhile. What he needed was an experienced manager who could devote time to him. Barney headed back to Chicago.

Some managers are greedy, pushing a fighter through the wringer in a furious flurry of matches that fatten the manager's bankroll but leave the boxer drained dry and gutted. Some are good, solid citizens who worry about the fighter's future, bringing him along slowly, conserving him, fine-tuning him for the long haul. Barney was lucky—he latched on to a managerial partnership in the latter category, Sam Pian and Art Winch. There was nothing they did not know about developing a boxer properly, and they had a reputation for integrity.

Pian and Winch laid out a no-nonsense schedule and held Barney to it. Mornings were devoted to roadwork, afternoons to calisthenics and bag-punching followed by a ring workout against accomplished sparring partners. Then it was home and early to bed. Art Winch supervised the training schedule and he was a hard taskmaster. He bore down especially on Barney's pacing—fighting in bursts and then laying back to collect energy for another offensive burst—and on his punching—getting the proper leverage into his blows so that a sharp punch placed just right could poleax an opponent. Barney was working harder than ever and it was starting to reflect in his performance.

His managers booked Barney into a series of preliminary fights, spacing them judiciously and selecting opponents carefully. He won almost all of them but Pian and Winch were still not satisfied. They could spot flaws in his performance. He had more to learn, more seasoning to get under his belt, and they did their best to provide it.

It was mid-1932 before his managers considered Barney really ready, and they booked him against Ray Miller, a top-ranking lightweight with a strong left hook. Miller used that hook with punishing effect, opening a deep gash in Barney's forehead in the third round. In the fourth Barney weaved in fast and caught Miller on the chin with a hard right that rocked him. From then on, Barney kept the pressure on Miller. In the late rounds Miller was too busy backpedaling to lash out with his hook. Barney won in a lopsided decision.

The slow build-up and long apprenticeship were over—Barney was on his way. In the fall he decisioned Bat Battalino, a former featherweight titleholder. Six months later he whipped Billy Petrolle, the leading light-weight contender. In beating Petrolle so decisively he emerged as the new leading contender for the lightweight crown. No other fighter stood between him and Tony Canzoneri, who held the lightweight and junior welterweight titles simultaneously. The match was booked.

This was a hectic period for Barney. He was busy preparing for the Canzoneri fight and busy redeeming the pledge he had made to himself nine years earlier when his father was murdered. Having finally accumulated sufficient money, he moved his mother into a larger apartment and then brought his sister and two younger brothers home from the orphanage. It had taken a long time and a lot of fights, but the years and the fights magically evaporated—the Rasofskys were reunited under the same roof once again.

With his family settled, Barney purged his mind of everything except the big fight. Canzoneri was a popular champ and masterful in the ring—tough and crafty, with speed, endurance, and a knockout punch. This would be by far the greatest test that Barney had faced.

Chicago Stadium was jammed that night in June, 1933. A roar went up when champion and challenger climbed through the ropes. The fight began at a furious pace that continued round after round as each pressed for advantage. Both of those weaving, darting, bobbing bodies were taking a pounding. Six rounds. Eight. Each fighter's face was now lacerated and bloody. Eleven rounds. Twelve. Both fighters, near exhaustion, still pressed in, trading blows. The crowd was frenzied. At the end of round fifteen both men were still on their feet but each was utterly spent. They awaited the verdict. The referee checked the judges and then raised Barney's hand in victory. He was the new lightweight and junior welterweight champion of the world.

The fact that the fight had been such a close thing bothered Barney. He wanted a clear-cut, decisive victory to silence any skeptics who thought he might have been the beneficiary of hometown bias. So he signed for a rematch in September in Canzoneri's hometown, New York, where nobody could claim the Chicagoan held an advantage.

The second fight was even more vicious than the first. Neither fighter tried to pace himself, to husband a reserve for later rounds. Each, striving for a quick kill, bore in relentlessly. It was combat on an elemental level and it electrified the jam-packed Polo Grounds. It ended like their first encounter—both of them bruised, bloody, and gasping, and Barney's hand raised in triumph. Now there could be no question of his right to the twin titles.

In less than a year Barney disposed of every serious contender and was hard-pressed to find a worthwhile opponent in his weight class. Turning aside the protests of his managers, he persuaded them to arrange a match with Jimmy McLarnin, the welterweight champion. This was a daring move—many called it foolhardy—because McLarnin, then in his prime, was an awesomely powerful fighter and Barney would be handing him a 10-pound advantage in a situation where every ounce of muscle would be a priceless asset.

The Ross-McLarnin fight made boxing history. Barney stood toe-to-toe trading blows with the heavier man, and if he had a shade less beef to put into his punches he had a shade more speed and accuracy. Barney took the decision and with it the welterweight crown to go along with his junior welterweight and lightweight titles. In all the annals of pugilism no man before him had ever held three crowns at the same time.

That fall there was a Ross-McLarnin rematch. It was close and the ringside judges split between the two opponents. The referee broke the tie by voting for McLarnin, and Barney became the ex-welterweight king. Six months later the pair clashed for the third time. Barney emerged from the encounter with a unanimous decision that restored his welterweight crown.

Since his first Canzoneri fight Barney had been earning good purses and he should have been rolling in money, but he wasn't. After he took care of his family's needs and his training expenses he took care of all of his friends and of the hordes of strangers who came to him with hard-luck stories. He had known poverty too intimately not to be a pushover for anyone in need. To compound the problem, he had discovered horses and whenever he could he visited the track where he invariably dropped a bundle. Yet, he wasn't worried. He was fighting often, bringing in new purses to replace the old ones slipping through his fingers.

Nothing lasts forever. For the champion the end came on May 31, 1938, when he was twenty-eight and a veteran of ten years of professional campaigning in which he had won 75 fights, drawn three, and lost three. His opponent that night was Henry Armstrong. Hammerin' Henry had earned his nickname by knocking out 29 of the 30 opponents he had vanquished. In 1938 Hammerin' Henry was at his peak, Barney Ross was past his. The disparity became evident before the fight had progressed very far.

The first two rounds were hard-fought but fairly even. In round three Barney showed a burst of his old speed and his old skills; that was his round, but it was the last one he could claim. From then on it was all Armstrong, punching without let-up, hammering his fists into the champ. By the time the fight was half over Barney was grotesquely battered and bloody, both eyes puffed and one completely shut, nose swollen to twice normal size, body a mass of ugly welts and bruises. The fans, usually yelling for blood, lapsed into silence at first, then—recoiling from the butchery—bellowed to referee Art Donovan to halt the savage spectacle. At the end of the 10th, Donovan had to guide the half-blind fighter back to his corner. "This is it," he told Barney. "I've got to stop it."

"I'm the champ; let me go out like one, let me go out fighting," Barney pleaded.

Pian and Winch, heartsick over the brutal beating, tried to reason with Barney but he was adamant. Reluctantly, Donovan agreed to hold off as long as he could. Pian and Winch averted their eyes from the ring as the fight continued.

In the final rounds, fighting on instinct and raw courage, Barney managed somehow to stay on his feet and even to try to press in on Armstrong. It was a remarkable performance and Hammerin' Henry, appreciating what it cost the fading champion, no longer tried for a knockout. It was a tribute from one great fighter to another. Barney Ross had been magnificent in victory. He was magnificent in defeat.

While Barney was mending in the weeks that followed,

promoters dangled offers before him for quick fights that would rake in money while his epic stand against Armstrong was still fresh in the minds of the fans. He refused them all. He was too proud to cash in on what used to be but could not be again.

After floundering for a bit while trying to figure out how a twenty-eight-year-old ex-champ makes a new life for himself, Barney opened a cocktail lounge in Chicago. The new venture thrived. Had the story ended there it still would have contained the elements that inspire—a scrawny, ghetto youngster equal to the burdens of a manhood thrust on him overnight, with the courage and fortitude to fight his way to the top, and with pride and dignity intact even in defeat. But the story does not end there.

When America was plunged into World War II, Barney Ross quietly wound up his business affairs to enlist in the Marines. Eleven months after Pearl Harbor, Private Ross—at thirty-three nearly twice as old as many of the Marines around him—waded ashore on Guadalcanal, a rugged, Japanese-held island in the southwest Pacific.

For the next six weeks the unit suffered heavy casualties as it inched forward against stiff Japanese resistance. In late December, Barney volunteered to scout ahead with a small patrol probing for enemy emplacements. After a deep penetration, the patrol was suddenly raked by bullets from the encircling jungle. The men dived into two nearby shell holes for cover. Barney eased his rifle over the rim of his shelter and began firing into the jungle. It was minutes before he realized he was the only Marine firing. A quick check revealed that his companions—three with him and two in the adjoining hole—

were so badly wounded they could not use their weapons. One of the men could manage to reload, and while Barney fired he prepared fresh weapons for him. The minutes stretched into an hour, and then a second hour.

When it became dark Barney scuttled to the next hole for more ammunition. The two men there were in bad shape and he did what he could for them before starting back with the precious ammo. He had almost made it when bullets ripped into his side and leg. Hurling himself into the hole, he tied hasty dressings over his wounds and resumed firing. As the night wore on, he tried to conserve his dwindling ammunition by spacing his shots and lobbing an occasional grenade to keep the Japanese pulled back. At some time during his ordeal he was hit again, this time in the ankle.

When the sky began to lighten, Barney braced himself. He knew daylight would bring a final attack to overrun him and the men he was trying to save. The attack came, but it was not the Japanese—it was a rescue mission routing the enemy! Barney Ross' longest night had finally ended.

It was after he was satisfied the patrol was safe that the waves of pain surged through Barney. His vision grew fuzzy and he began to shake uncontrollably. He thought the shakes were simply a reaction, but the medics discovered that he had been walking around with a case of malaria and had a high fever. They treated his wounds, dosed him, and gave him an injection that brought relief.

The need for men up on the line was so great that before he had fully recovered Barney was back in combat. His wounds still pained him and the malarial attacks were striking with growing frequency and intensity. After several weeks he was evacuated to a base hospital for further treatment.

It was clear to the doctors that Barney had kept going on willpower and his ability to absorb punishment. He was racked with fever, his wounds throbbed maddeningly, malaria and dysentery tormented him. To relieve him, the hospital staff dosed him with morphine. It eased the pain and for the first time in two months Barney was free of his agony—until the morphine wore off. The medics gave him another shot. And then another. And again. Neither they, nor he, realized they were saddling him with an even greater torture, the torture of drug addiction. When Barney walked off the Navy hospital ship in California in 1943 he had several souvenirs of Guadalcanal: corporal's stripes, the Silver Star for heroism, and a tormented body that cried out for the release that came in a syringe of morphine.

Ashore, Barney found private doctors who, unaware of his addiction, gave him morphine to ease his obvious pain. Meanwhile, Navy doctors treated the damage that was apparent to them—the wounds, the persistent malaria, the general exhaustion and combat fatigue. When they could do no more, they gave him a medical discharge from the Marines.

Shackled by his body's insistent craving for narcotics, Barney made the rounds of doctors' offices until he ran out of sympathetic doctors. Then, hating himself but powerless to resist, he found a dope pusher in Los Angeles from whom he could make buys. After that, wherever he went he found a pusher eager to supply him—for a price. Barney suffered the agony of the damned. He cursed the pushers who were driving him into debt to satisfy his hunger, cursed himself even more for submitting to his craving. Anguished, he suffered alone as he strived to keep his terrible burden secret from family and friends.

In mid-1946 Barney Ross made a decision that required as much courage and determination as he had ever displayed in the ring or on Guadalcanal. He voluntarily turned himself in to federal authorities as an addict, in order to undergo treatment. He knew what he faced: public exposure, humiliation, the ordeal of being cut off from the drugs his body demanded. But he also knew that life would not be worth living if he could not regain the self-respect that his addiction had stolen.

As the hospital staff withdrew Barney from drugs his body burned with consuming fever, his stomach knotted and heaved, his torso jerked convulsively, his mind reeled with shattering nightmares. Through it all Barney clutched desperately to one thought: his absolute, bedrock need to defeat the devil in his flesh. Never had he faced a more vicious enemy; never had he fought so hard.

The first few weeks were the worst. After he had battled his way past the crisis, the strain of withdrawal diminished and the doctors could commence therapy to rebuild the ravaged patient. In early 1947 it was clear that Barney Ross had won his battle. The hospital closed out his file and discharged him. Barney felt that he had been reborn. In a sense, he had.

Having suffered the scourge of addiction and beaten it, he felt a deep concern for those still enslaved by drugs. Wherever he went, Barney sought out addicts and those taking the first steps toward addiction. He reasoned with them, persuaded, pleaded, counselled, encouraged. His words carried weight because he spoke from the depths of bitter experience. Nobody knows how many victims he rescued from the enemy within.

When Barney had been a neophyte boxer his fans in Chicago used to say he had "moxie." That word has gone out of fashion, but it means courage, guts, determination, a refusal to accept defeat. It is too bad the word is no longer current; it is such a perfect way to describe Barney Ross—in the ring or out.

2   The Incomparable Babe

Babe Didrikson

O<small>N</small> SEPTEMBER 27, 1956, President Eisenhower held one of his regularly scheduled press conferences. He revealed no startling news to the journalists, produced no grist for the mills of future historians, yet the conference established a Presidential precedent. No President before him, and none since, has ever opened a press conference as he did that day—by paying tribute to an athlete. But then, never before or since has there been an athlete quite like Babe Didrikson Zaharias.

Even when she was simply Mildred Didrikson—a preschooler in her native Beaumont, Texas—it was clear that she and athletics were made for each other. A home-made backyard gym, cleverly fashioned by her father from scrap, was the place where it began. Here was a fascinating array of things to scramble over, to tug on, to climb, to lift. By the time she entered school she had become surprisingly adept on the apparatus.

While other girls her age were passing through their doll-cuddling phase, Mildred was developing strength and agility on the home-made athletic equipment. Even-

tually the backyard gym was no longer enough for her—
she felt a need to compete, to pit herself against people
instead of props.

The most readily available competitive sport was the
neighborhood baseball game. Mildred watched the best
players closely, practicing their movements in private
until she had the hang of them. Then she commenced
pestering the boys for admission to their game. They
closed ranks against a girl with the temerity to try to in-
vade the male world of baseball. However, Mildred's persistence wore them down and in the end their resistance
collapsed.

Mildred played well enough for a beginner, but as she
gained experience she improved steadily. Soon she
ranked up with the best of the sandlotters. There was
confidence in her fielding and she ran the bases with
flair. It was her batting, though, that really brought the
house down. The long ball became her trademark and
she became known through the neighborhood for the
homers she walloped so frequently. The other players
began to call her Babe, after Babe Ruth. The name took
hold and even to her family she was Babe from then on.

In junior high Babe went out for basketball and made
the girls' squad, but when she reached high school and
the coach took one look at her—then a shade under five
feet tall and barely 100 pounds—he turned away, unim-
pressed. "Too small to make it in high school competition," he said.

Babe was deflated, not defeated. She continued to work
out by herself and to study the finer points of the game.
She was particularly attentive when the boys' team was in
action because their brand of ball—fast, hard-fought, de-

ceptive—excited her. She taught herself to duplicate their techniques and to play their aggressive kind of game. And she kept after the coach for a tryout. In the 1930 season, when Babe was fifteen, the coach gave her her chance. From the outset she was impressive and it earned her a berth on the team. As the season wore on she blossomed into a dazzling player, dribbling rings around the bigger girls, pivoting out of their reach, shooting baskets cleanly from midcourt or from under the backboard. Her timing was split-second, her accuracy almost flawless, and she became the highest scoring member of the team. Sports buffs in Beaumont began to sing Babe's praises and their song was heard in the front office of Employers Casualty Company in Dallas.

The insurance company, very big on employee teams as a morale booster and as a form of advertising, offered Babe a job. She accepted it and the office duties and basketball uniform that went with it. The following month Employees Casualty made it to the finals of the Women's National AAU tournament with Babe playing as a regular. The team lost the finals by a single point, but it came away with the title the following year and came within a whisker of repeating its championship the next year too. In all three years Babe, the team high-scorer, was named to the women's All-American basketball team.

It is too long from one basketball season to the next for someone as enamored of sports as Babe. That first between-seasons summer with Employees Casualty she was on the company swimming and diving team and played on the softball team. That was also the summer in which she saw her first track and field meet. She was surprised by it—she had not realized there were so many different types of track and field events. Until then, Employees Casualty had not had a women's track and field team, but at Babe's urging the front office agreed to start one.

As with every sport she ever tackled, Babe approached track and field as though it were a personal challenge she was honor-bound to subdue. She hung on every word of advice from the coaches, assimilating it carefully and depositing it in her memory bank like an account to be drawn on in time of stress. Above all, she practiced. Team practice was scheduled for one hour each afternoon but she returned to the field alone each evening for an additional two-hour workout.

In 1931 Babe was a member of the Employees Casualty team that competed in the Women's National AAU championships in Jersey City, placing first in the broad jump, baseball throw, and 80-meter hurdles, setting new world records in the throw and the hurdles. After her sparkling AAU performance she did not relax her rigid schedule because she had a fresh goal in mind: the 1932 Olympics.

The steppingstone to the Olympics was to be the women's combined national championships and Olympic trials in track and field in Evanston, Illinois. When the double-barrelled meet came up in July, 1932, Babe was ready for it, trained to a fine edge. The real question was whether or not the meet was ready for her. The question was relevant because Babe was to constitute the *entire* Employees Casualty team. As the teams were announced they trotted out on the field—anywhere from a dozen to two dozen to a team—to take their bows. A buzz rippled through the stands when Employees Casualty was announced over the PA and Babe trotted out all alone.

The meet got under way and the one-girl team rushed from event to event. She threw the discus, hurried over to run a heat in the 80-meter hurdles, took her turn at the broad jump, hustled over to put the 8-pound shot, tossed the javelin, threw the baseball, and then scurried about repeating her circuit in the next round of those events. It was an unprecedented performance.

Babe nailed down first in the broad jump, the shot put, the baseball throw, the hurdles, and the javelin toss—the last two with new world marks. In only one event, the 100-meter dash, did she fail to score. All alone she amassed a total of 30 points to win the team championship. Second place went to the 22-member Illinois Women's Athletic Club team with 22 points, an average of one point per contestant stacked up against Babe's 30 points. The one-woman team from Dallas had had a Roman holiday and the crowd loved it.

Two weeks later when the stringy, eighteen-year-old phenomenon arrived in Los Angeles for the 1932 Olympics she was under the gun, bird-dogged by both rooters who thought she could do no wrong and by skeptics who were sure she must be a flash in the pan. She entered the maximum allowable number of events for a single athlete—three: javelin, hurdles, and high jump.

It was late on the opening day before Babe's first event was called: the javelin throw. She rifled her javelin with a heave that carried it 143 feet and 4 inches, a new world record. That great effort extracted its price—a painfully torn cartilage in her right shoulder. Saying nothing, because if she did not take her two follow-up tosses she would be automatically eliminated, Babe ignored the pain and heaved twice more, but both attempts fell short of her original mark. However, none of the other contestants could match her original toss and she walked away with the first-place gold medal.

On the second day Babe ran the qualifying heat in the 80-meter hurdles in the record time of 11.8 seconds. In the finals she flashed across the finish line in even faster time—11.7 seconds—to take her second gold medal.

An emotional charge crackled around the stadium the next day. Could Babe make a clean sweep of her three events by winning the high jump?

In 1932 the world record for the women's high jump stood at 5 feet, 3 inches. The crossbar was moved up progressively until—at the 5-5 level—there were only two contestants left to battle it out: Babe Didrikson and Jean Shiley. Both jumped successfully and the bar was raised another three-quarters of an inch. Shiley tried and missed. Babe leaped and cleared the bar but coming down she grazed one of the uprights enough to jiggle the crossbar loose. The officials lowered it a half inch and both girls tried again. Shiley jumped first and made it. Babe also sailed over the bar cleanly. But the judge disallowed Babe's jump, ruling that her head crossed over before her feet—in those days not permissible although it is allowed today. Babe had to content herself with the second-place silver to go along with the two first-place golds she had won.

Back in Dallas, Babe was given a heroine's welcome. She walked on air for a day or two and then looked for new athletic fields to conquer. She found her next challenge when she tried a few rounds of golf and was smitten with the game. Those who witnessed her first tentative forays into the new sport were impressed with the distance she got in her drives. Babe was not misled by those powerful drives; she was athlete enough to know that nobody muscles his way to the top of any sport on sheer brawn alone. She realized how much she would have to learn about the game and its finer points, how hard she would have to practice if she were to master it. The challenge appealed to her.

Babe never believed in halfway measures. That spring, having saved up a nest egg to tide her over, she went to California to concentrate on becoming a golfer. Until her money ran out she lived golf each day, practicing diligently under the guidance of professional teachers. Then, to pump new blood into her anemic finances, she barnstormed successively with a girls' basketball team and a men's baseball team and ultimately wound up in her old insurance company job in Dallas. Resuming her golf lessons, she practiced on the local course before going to the office and again each day after work. When her fingers split open from the beating they were taking, as they often did, she taped them and kept going.

In late 1934 Babe entered her first tournament, the Fort Worth Women's Invitational. She was eliminated in match play but not before she had won a medal in the qualifying round with a respectable 77. A few months later she was back in tournament play, this time seeking even bigger game: the Texas State women's championship.

She made it through the qualifying round, the quarter-finals, and the semifinals. In the payoff round she was pitted against Peggy Chandler, a tough competitor who had finished either first or second in each of the prior three years. Initially, Babe pulled ahead; then Chandler drew even and passed her. On the 23rd hole she was three strokes up on Babe but by the 33rd both players were tied. On the 34th, Babe sank an eagle-three for a one-stroke advantage, and on the 36th she added another one-stroke advantage to collar the Texas championship. The lithe, green-eyed athlete had just turned twenty-one and was achieving distinction in yet another sport.

Golf now became Babe's major activity. She devoted the next two years to rigorous practice and to tournament play. This time her money worries were minimal because a sporting goods house paid her a retainer for permission to market clubs bearing her name.

In 1938 Babe entered the Los Angeles Open. She didn't get a win out of it but she came away with a husband-to-be, George Zaharias, a professional wrestler she met on the course. Two days before Christmas they married. The honeymoon was delayed until the following spring but when it came there was nothing routine about it. The Zahariases sailed for Australia where George booked wrestling matches for himself and golf exhibitions for Babe. It isn't every American bride who spends her honeymoon golfing her way around Australia.

During World War II Babe's golf was largely confined to benefit exhibitions for war charities. In one of these, Bob Hope made the widely quoted comment that the only difference between his game and Babe's was that he hit the ball like a girl and she swung like a man. It was more than a comic crack; it was an astute observation of Babe's style of play. She hit the ball in great, arching drives that boomed out, eating up distance. It was these drives that helped her win the Western Women's Open in 1944 and to defend the title successfully the following year.

Relentless in the pursuit of excellence, Babe fought for every hole, putting out the best of which she was capable, even though she might already have the game won. She didn't believe in coasting or in bringing in cheap victories. Of all the tales about her that fans love to recount, one in particular illustrates the character of her game admirably. She had been leading in a tournament when she discovered she had played the wrong ball out of the rough. She could have continued play, because she alone knew of the error, but she reported it to the officials to disqualify herself.

"You could have gone on," a bystander chided. "Nobody would have known the difference."

Her reply tells a lot about Babe. "I'd have known the difference. You have to play golf by the rules just as you have to live by the rules of life. There is no other way."

In 1946, the war over, golf throttled up to a full slate of tournaments. In the next few months Babe won five straight contests, including the National, the big one on the slate. By May of 1947 she had run her unbroken string of wins to 15. It was then that George Zaharias proposed that she play the British Women's Amateur in Scotland in June. Since the classic began in 1893 no American woman had ever won it. This was the kind of challenge she thrived on. She decided to enter.

On the first day of play on the tricky Scottish course Babe won her two matches, and her two on the second. On the third day she took the morning match against stubborn opposition and then breezed through the afternoon contest. Matters came to a head on the fourth day when she faced Jacqueline Gordon in the finals.

Through the morning both women played neck and neck, each carding a 75. After the lunch break Babe began to pull ahead. She had the touch—the ball was doing what she wanted it to do. Play ended with Babe up five strokes to become the first American ever to wear the British women's crown. When she sailed home a boatload of reporters and photographers steamed out of New York harbor to escort her in.

Babe was America's darling. Even those who customarily skipped the sports pages hailed her accomplishment. Now, more than ever, she was in demand for exhibitions, matches, promotions of all kinds. Babe pushed herself trying to satisfy all the demands placed on her. In 1948 the strain began to tell—she developed an erratic pain in her left side. The pain would come, accompanied by a swelling, and then both pain and swelling would subside. She knew she should see a doctor but could not seem to find the time, so she continued her hectic pace and tried not to think of the pain that came and went.

Midway through a tournament in Seattle in 1952 the pain became so intense she could no longer ignore it. Babe flew to her family doctor in Beaumont and he discovered that she had a strangulated hernia. He ordered immediate surgery.

Three months later Babe was back in competition, this time in the tough Tam O'Shanter. Still weak, going into the final nine holes she was bone-weary; coming out, she was glassy-eyed. Still, she managed a third-place finish. By October, when she won the Texas Women's Open, she was feeling stronger and playing better. But the spell of well-being was brief. Going into the 1953 tournament circuit she found she was dragging herself around the course, wondering if she could make it to the final hole.

The circuit moved to Babe's hometown, Beaumont, in April for the Babe Zaharias Open, named in her honor. She was determined to play in it, though from the very first tee it was torture for her. Nevertheless, she willed herself to continue and she even managed to bring off the victory.

The next morning she was in her doctor's office when he arrived. He kept her in the examination room for a long time and then sent her to a specialist who confirmed his shattering diagnosis: cancer. Babe was immediately hospitalized for a colostomy, major surgery in which the intestines are diverted to discharge body wastes through an opening cut into the flesh. A week later, when Babe was for the first time permitted out of bed for a few minutes, she swayed against the nurse supporting her, realizing how weak the operation had left her. Back in bed, she commenced a routine of prone exercises that she was to continue for the rest of her hospital stay—an alternate flexing and relaxing of her arm and leg muscles. Lying there trying to coax some vigor back into her limbs, Babe also forced herself to adjust to the fact that henceforth she would have to live with a pouch fastened to her side to collect her body waste. She was resolved that she would not fall victim to the mental depression that afflicts many who undergo colostomies. Forty-three days after her operation she was permitted to return home.

Within days the indomitable Babe reached for her clubs and began to practice simple chip shots and putts. Gradually, she worked herself up to her woods. At the same time, she followed a schedule of calisthenics that increased in intensity as strength began to return to her. Three-and-a half months after the surgery she entered the Tam O'Shanter. Before it ended she was ashen-faced from fatigue but she would not quit and she captured third place. The time had not yet come to write her off as a has-been.

Ten months after the colostomy Babe won her first major tournament since the operation. She played well for the balance of the year, winning several more tournaments. But if she had regained her old skill she had not regained her old stamina. She felt exhausted much of the time. Even so, she refused to let her weariness keep her from a heavy schedule of personal appearances in behalf of cancer drives.

Husband, family, and friends urged Babe to stop punishing herself, to conserve her strength. "After all," they would reason with her, "you have nothing more to prove. You have proved everything that any athlete could hope to."

"But now there is something else I have to do," Babe would insist. "Now I have to give hope to other cancer victims. I have to keep demonstrating that you can come back from cancer to do whatever you did before and to do it well."

Babe started 1955 by winning the Tampa Women's Open. Then, she had a new cross to bear: an agonizing pain in her spinal column. After the pain appeared she played in three more tournaments—winning one—before she took time out to consult doctors. They found that she had a ruptured spinal disc; once again she was on the operating table. Even before scar tissue had formed over this latest of her surgical ordeals, the doctors discovered that her cancer had returned. From then on Babe was in and out of the hospital for X-ray treatments in a bid to halt the ravages of the disease. Through it all she bore up like the phenomenal champion she was—with quiet courage and dignity. Between hospital visits she continued to play golf and to support cancer drives.

By mid-1956 the truth was evident to everyone except Babe. She simply refused to concede defeat. In July she underwent yet another major operation, a chordotomy to sever the spinal nerves to block off the excruciating pains in her lower body. Despite everything, Babe showed no self-pity, even attempting to cheer up her visitors if she felt they were downcast.

On September 27, 1956, Babe Didrikson Zaharias died as she had lived—a champion. Later that day, when President Eisenhower commenced his press conference with a tribute to Babe and her rare courage, none of the assembled reporters thought it strange.

3   Howe, and How!

Gordie Howe

SLASHING STICKS and flashing blades, hurtling pucks and rocketing skaters, crackling slap shots and bruising body checks—that's ice hockey, a violent, lightning-fast game that assaults the senses with its intensity. Clearly, the professional hockey rink is no place for the shy or for the aged. Which makes the sport's most brilliant star an oddity on both counts.

Holder of all the records in the book, balding Gordie Howe—born in Saskatoon, Canada, in 1928—is an amazing grandfather who has spent more years in the ice wars than any other professional player in history and is still a powerhouse on skates. Equally startling, decades of pro hockey mayhem have not erased his soft-spoken, unassuming modesty, his gentle sense of humor, or the lingering traces of his boyhood shyness. It was that shyness, in fact, that was almost his undoing at the very beginning of his career.

It isn't true that all Canadian youngsters are born with ice skates on their feet; it only seems that way. Gordie Howe had to wait until he was five to get his first pair of skates—worn and rusted, secondhand relics. Those were Depression days and it was the best his unemployed father could provide. Since his hand-me-down skates were a couple of sizes too large for him he had to wear several pairs of thick socks to fill in the gaps.

The winter freeze comes early and stays late in Saskatoon, so that ice is the hub around which the region's outdoor life revolves. That was a circumstance that pleased Gordie because it was on the ice that he released his pent-up energy and found thrills to counterbalance the quiet, orderly routine of everyday life. Whenever he had a free moment during those long winter months of his childhood he was on his cherished blades playing hockey, or doing endurance skating to build up leg muscles, or practicing sprints, quick turns, and stick handling. By the time he reached his early teens it was clear to everyone that he had a great talent for the sport. Big for his age, he skated with a natural sense of balance, with grace, and with long, powerful strides that swept him across the ice with remarkable speed. A brainy player, resourceful whether on offense or defense, he had quick reflexes and his stickwork was consistently accurate. In 1953 he was spotted by a scout for the New York Rangers and, though Gordie was only fifteen, he was invited to the team's tryout camp in Winnipeg.

It was Gordie Howe's first trip away from home; Winnipeg, so big and bustling after Saskatoon, overwhelmed him. Older, more city-wise novices at the camp, taking advantage of Gordie's lack of sophistication, made him the butt of their jokes. When he was confronted for the first time with the complicated pads and protectors that professionals wear, he didn't know how to suit up properly and this provoked an outburst of heckling and teasing that made Gordie's embarrassment acute. He had never felt so alone and friendless. Homesick for family and more familiar, more gentle surroundings, after five days he returned to Saskatoon.

The following year Gordie was "rediscovered" by a scout, this time from the Detroit Red Wings. The scout persuaded Gordie to visit the team's tryout camp in Windsor, Ontario, and this time he knew what to expect, so he was prepared for it. Going through his paces out on the ice, he overcame his initial nervousness and his acute awareness of the critical eyes scrutinizing his moves. He was impressive, demonstrating that he had the skills and the potential to make good—given proper coaching and a cushion of experience. Because he was too young at just sixteen for professional play, the Detroit management assigned him to an Ontario amateur team for seasoning.

A year of hard work and astute coaching in the Ontario league brought Gordie along soundly, adding enough polish to his game to convince the Detroit management to try him in professional competition. They signed him on with their farm team in Omaha in the old United States Hockey League.

The transition from amateur to professional hockey is a rude awakening for rookies. It isn't just that the caliber of pro play is so much better, so much faster, wilier, and more skillful. It is also that for the professional the game is a job as well as a sport, and competition for that all-important paycheck is an incentive that escalates play to a level of ferocity unknown in amateur rinks. Rookies discover the hard way what it is to be speared and hacked and hooked with the stick, to be slammed into the boards savagely, to be on the receiving end of punishing strategems designed to intimidate and neutralize them. For many, the constant battering and the unrelenting strain turn out to be more than they can handle.

Gordie took his lumps and coped. He learned how to protect himself without sacrificing his game, adjusting to the wide-open, aggressive play of the pros. By season's end he had racked up a respectable total of 48 points—22 goals and 26 assists.

Though he was maturing on the ice, off it he was still the shy, small-town youth. On the team's first road trip to Minneapolis, when dinner time arrived Gordie peeked into the hotel dining room and was dismayed to discover how elegant and cosmopolitan it seemed. Abashed by the grandeur of the setting, he went to a nearby drugstore where he sat at the counter drinking a milk shake. With only that insubstantial pregame snack to sustain him he still managed to score two goals that evening.

In 1946 Gordie Howe moved up to the Detroit Red Wings from the Omaha farm club. He was eighteen now and had reached his full growth: six feet, 200 pounds, with the big, sloping shoulders and long arms that are such an asset in hockey. Playing right wing for Detroit, he was awed to be in the National Hockey League skating against the best, the toughest competition in the sport. He knew that he could not relax, that he would have to prove his right to remain in the big time. So he practiced indefatigably, studied the play of the older, more experienced skaters to learn what he could from them, pored over game films to see what was effective and what was not, hung onto every word of advice from the coaches, lived and breathed the sport. The unremitting effort was reflected in his performance. Week by week he was playing the wingman's slot with greater competence and assurance.

Accustomed by now to the very physical style of pro play, Gordie had learned to live with the aches and pains that he accumulated as the season wore on. In a game against Toronto he was battling Gus Mortson for the puck when Mortson's elbow slammed into his mouth, smashing three of his front teeth out of his jaw. It was the first of many permanent scars he would bear as mementos of the rink.

The 1949–50 season marked Gordie's coming-of-age in the National Hockey League. Earlier he had been a subtle, controlled player whose moves were characterized by speed, finesse, and remarkable eye-hand-foot coordination. He had built on the subtlety of his game, adapting it to the NHL's pugnacious play without destroying it. The opposition could no longer ride him off the puck, bull him into the boards, or check him with impunity. But the opposition also discovered that Gordie could think on the run. He had become a master tactician able to set up and direct a pattern of play, able to screen his shots skillfully and fake out the other side, able to read a rival's strategy and instantly devise effective countermoves.

In regular season play that year he amassed a total of 68 points, which put him up among the league's leaders. Fans hailed Howe for his rink performance and for his off-the-ice quiet modesty, a refreshing novelty in the brash world of hockey. Knowledgeable observers, appreciating the fine points of Howe's game, marked him for greatness. Then, in one stunning blow, all speculation about his future was reduced to a single, stark question of survival.

It happened in a hard-fought game against the Toronto Maple Leafs in the postseason Stanley Cup playoffs in Detroit's Olympia Stadium. Ted Kennedy of the Leafs was streaking down the ice, adroitly maneuvering the puck before him. Howe raced in to check him. The two collided like express trains at full throttle. Howe crumpled to the ice against the boards in front of the Wings' bench. He lay motionless in a twisted heap, blood spurting from his right eye and puddling around him. The crowded stadium was hushed as the unconscious wingman was carried off to a hastily summoned ambulance.

A quick survey was all the surgeons at Harper Hospital needed to recognize that they faced an immense challenge. In addition to the severely damaged eye, Howe had sustained multiple broken bones, including various facial fractures, but most frightening of all was a massive concussion exerting pressure against the brain. Moving swiftly, the surgeons began drilling into his head in an effort to relieve the pressure that could destroy the brain.

The tragedy had shocked players and fans alike. After Howe had been carried from the stadium the game resumed on a somber note. Howe's teammates, determined to pull off a victory for him, played with quiet fury and took the game. Then all Detroit gathered around its radios for the half-hourly medical bulletins the city's stations broadcast throughout the night. It was well into the next day before it was clear that—barring complications—Howe would live. But would he ever lace on skates again? Few people, including his surgeons, thought it likely.

Once Howe had turned the corner, his superbly conditioned body began the task of repairing itself. In the meantime the Red Wings, having eliminated the Maple Leafs from Stanley Cup contention, went up against the Rangers in the finals. When the see-saw battle moved down to the game in which the Wings could sew up the cup, Detroit's Olympia Stadium was jammed. Among the fired-up spectators was Gordie Howe, pale and wearing a hat to hide the nakedness of a head that had not yet regrown the hair shaved off for his surgery. Playing at the top of their form, the Red Wings won the game.

When the Wings lined up at center ice to receive the Stanley Cup, shouts for Howe to take his place with the team echoed through the stadium. Embarrassed by the furor, he went out on the ice, moving gingerly on the slippery surface. As the players clustered around him, one of them snatched off Howe's hat to expose his scarred, hairless head. The fans erupted in a wild, sustained ovation. If this were to be the last time they would see Howe on the ice, as most assumed, they were out to make it a memorable occasion. But Howe was determined that this would not be his swan song. He meant to be back.

Throughout the summer Howe worked on a conditioning program, each day extending himself to a higher level of performance. He had feared that his damaged eye would so distort his vision that it would ruin the accuracy of his passing shots and scoring drives; to his profound relief this turned out not to be so. When the Wings opened training camp in September, there was Number 9—Gordie Howe—suited up and ready to go. When league play commenced he was at his accustomed right wing position, skating better than ever. He ended the season with 86 points, more than any other NHL player had ever scored in a single season.

After the final game Howe returned to the hospital, this time for operations on both knees to try to undo the damage inflicted on them by slashing sticks. Again he spent the summer on a reconditioning program and again, when the new season opened, he was performing better than ever. Once more he led the league in scoring, with 86 points to match his record-setting 1951 total. In addition, he won the Hart trophy, the most distinguished individual award in pro hockey.

For several reasons 1953 was a vintage year for the Detroit right winger. Playing superbly, his score for the season was a remarkable 95 points, breaking the league record that he himself had set earlier. Once more he was awarded the Hart trophy. (Eventually he would win it more often than any man in NHL history.) And before the year was out he married a Detroit girl who, until the time a mutual friend introduced the couple at a bowling alley, had never seen a hockey game. His wife, Colleen, made up for lost time rapidly, becoming a very discerning and enthusiastic fan.

Most players have about seven good years in the NHL, seldom more than eight. After that, drained by the constant pressure and battered by the violence of the game, they are usually muscled off the ice by younger men hungry for their chance to make it to the top. But in 1954, eight years after joining the Red Wings, Howe dominated the sport as no player before him had.

Graceful as well as lightning-fast, his moves were supple, controlled. He pivoted, changed direction, shifted laterally with rare ease and rapidity. As a playmaker and puck-carrier, Howe was superb. He had the knack of maneuvering the puck before him on his stick without once taking his eyes off the other players to glance down at it, guiding it on instinct and peripheral vision alone. His slap shots—whipping his stick down from waist-height to burn the puck across the ice at speeds clocked as high as 120 miles an hour—were awesome. Adding a wrinkle that others tried to copy, he invented a variation of the usual slap shot that caught the opposition by surprise because it abandoned the telltale waist-high move and relied on powerful wrist action alone. Howe also devised new patterns of play that have since become standard. Before him, for instance, strategy was built around position-play maneuvering; but under his leadership the Wings broke with tradition, sending the forwards sweeping down the ice in crisscrossing moves to seek targets of opportunity. The innovation multiplied pressure on the opposition, creating scoring opportunities and bringing fresh excitement to the rink.

Lionized by fans and press, Howe never became quite comfortable with all the adulation, never forgot that he was part of a team. He pressed for openings to pass off to his teammates, setting them up for scores. His passes to them were crisp and sure whether delivered forehand or backhand, and he was ambidextrous to boot, so that if he could lay his stick on the puck he could get it to a teammate.

Legends about Gordie Howe were being woven into the fabric of the sport and every fan had his favorite anecdote. Perhaps most revealing of the character of the

man is the one involving Gump Worsley, one-time
Ranger goalie. In a Red Wing-Ranger game Worsley
knocked down the puck as it was about to loft over his
shoulder into the net behind him. In the process the
goalie fell, crashing on the ice heavily, the puck only a
couple of inches from his face. As Worsley lay spread-
eagled helplessly, wind knocked out of him, both teams
rushed in for the kill, sticks upraised for a smash that
could take the puck—and the goalie's head along with it.
Howe got there first. He had a sure shot into the net but
he ignored it; instead, he used his body as a shield to hold
off the other players long enough for Worsley to recover
from his precarious position. Howe was out to beat the
opposition, not to butcher it.

Howe was not as fortunate in shielding himself from
the crippling blows that make hockey such a high-risk
sport. His ribs have been broken three times, his shoulder
has been dislocated, his wrist has been broken, several of
his toes have been fractured. In one season alone doctors
needed 50 stitches to close gashes in his face; so many
stitches have been needed so often to repair facial damage that it has become difficult for surgeons to get a
needle through his scarred skin.

What kept Howe coming back for more year after year,
despite the mauling he was taking, was that the fascina-
tion and excitement of hockey never diminished for him,
the records that fell to his prowess never lost their ability
to thrill him. Another thing that kept hockey fresh and
alive for him was that his love for the ice had rubbed off
on his two sons—Marty, born in 1954, and Mark, born
the following year. When he skated with his sons, guiding

and coaching them or simply cavorting with them, he forgot the scars and the mounting years.

The inevitable happened in 1971. Though he was still a formidable player, Gordie Howe was now forty-three. He knew the Detroit management had to build for the future, so he bowed out to make room for a younger player. Howe had played in 1,687 games in a NHL career that spanned 25 seasons; no other man in the annals of the sport had come close to matching that record. He had scored 786 goals, 1,023 assists, and 1,809 points, and nobody had approached that either. Fans said that hockey would never again see his like.

But Howe was not yet through with hockey. For two years he chafed in retirement from the rink and then in 1973 the Houston Aeros of the World Hockey Association offered him a playing contract. Houston also wanted Mark and Marty to join the team. The chance to return to the rink and to play on the same team as his sons was irresistible to the elder Howe, despite the handicap of his long layoff. So he returned to the ice and, magically, the rust of two years flaked away. Old Number 9 demonstrated that he was still a powerhouse on blades—he ended the season with the league's Most Valuable Player award and berths on four WHA all-star teams.

For four seasons the first father-sons playing trio in hockey history brought fans flocking to Aeros' games and none went away disappointed. In 1977, when their Houston contracts expired, the three Howes accepted an attractive offer to play for the New England Whalers. It was as a Whaler on December 7 in a game against the Birmingham Bulls that Gordie Howe picked off a rebound and drilled the puck into the net for his 1,000th career goal, the first player ever to reach that incredible total. For that feat he was presented a gold puck.

Although he has shattered more records and set more precedents than any other player ever to lace up skates, Gordie Howe has one special favorite. It happened in a Whalers-Washington Capitals game in 1978. Midway in the second period came the most remarkable moment professional hockey has witnessed. Snaring the puck on his stick, Number 5 passed off to Number 18 who passed off to Number 9 who drilled it into the net—Mark Howe to Marty Howe to Gordie Howe for a Whaler goal. Fifty-year-old Gordie Howe, the patched-together grandfather who is probably the finest all-around player the game will ever see, bear-hugged his two sons while the stands erupted in pandemonium.

4   Ain't It a Blip?

Althea Gibson

MUDDY IN WINTER, dusty in summer, dirt-poor in all seasons, Silver, South Carolina, where Althea Gibson was born in 1927 was a few ramshackle, frame buildings too set in their ways to collapse and too ashamed of their appearance to stand straight.

Althea's parents, Daniel and Annie Gibson, sharecropped a small, leached-out farm that provided a barely marginal existence. For the cotton-chopping, work-worn blacks of Silver life was bleak and the future promised no better. Daniel Gibson thought that the prospects had to be brighter up north because they surely couldn't be dimmer, so he sent Althea ahead to live with his sister-in-law in Harlem while he tried to scrape up enough so that he and Annie could follow. It was a long time before the Gibsons were finally resettled under their own roof.

Dreams faded fast in the demoralizing misery of Harlem. Harlem was still Silver, only on a bigger, more hectic scale. Life was just as mean and frustrating and had to be fought just as hard. As soon as she was old enough to roam the seamy sidewalks and back alleys, Althea became a knowing spectator of Harlem's pathetic parade of wretchedness and blighted hopes, of grinding poverty and anguish. Observing it all, she became street-wise, distrustful, rebellious, defiant, vowing to herself that she would not be devoured by that jungle meekly and submissively.

Althea loathed school. It represented "authority" with its prohibitions, regulations, and myopia. The classroom taught abstractions and principles inconsistent with the realities she saw all around her and the teachers demanded obedience she was not prepared to give. She commenced playing hooky. When she did favor the classroom with one of her infrequent appearances the teachers gave her a tongue-lashing, occasionally reinforced with a spanking, that only hardened her dislike for school and pushed her into a shell of sullenness.

The Harlem streets became Althea's home-away-from-home and school-away-from-school. She learned how to use her fists and to scrounge nickels to escape to the dream-world of the movies; when there were no nickels she found ways to sneak in. And she played ball, any kind of ball that was available. She was growing into a tall, strong, gangling girl with the muscles and reflexes for sports and an aggressive drive to beat the competition. She played fast, hard-charging basketball on a neighborhood court. She hustled at stickball, a street version of baseball that calls for a broomstick, a rubber ball, and an ability to disappear fast if the ball breaks a window. And she was a standout at paddle tennis.

Paddle tennis, a cut-down form of conventional tennis, is played with a short-handled, solid paddle on a court that is only half the traditional size. During the summer the block on which the Gibsons lived was set aside by police as a play-street barred to traffic. Paddle tennis courts were painted over the road, and a city recreation aide provided paddles and balls and tried to keep things moving smoothly. Althea doted on the game because it gave her a chance to abandon herself in fierce one-on-one play.

Althea had become a hooky-playing, fun-seeking, authority-flouting, ball-happy roughneck. To everyone's surprise, including her own, she was graduated from junior high school despite her chronic truancy. Because she hadn't yet reached legal school-leaving age she enrolled in a vocational school. For a few months she attended fairly regularly, then she resumed her old pattern of truancy. To avoid clashes at home, and the spankings that inevitably followed a visit by the truant officer, she began spending a night or two in a girlfriend's house whenever she sensed domestic storms brewing. Sometimes when a friendly refuge was not available she spent the night riding the subway, dozing fitfully as the train squealed its endless round-trip to nowhere.

In the summer of 1941 the recreation department assigned Buddy Walker to supervise the play-street in Althea's block. He quickly became aware of Althea and her skillful, aggressive play at paddle tennis. She won the block championship and then beat the champions of neighboring streets. Walker suspected that, given the training, she would give a good account of herself on a regular tennis court. To find out, he dug into his own pocket and bought her a used but serviceable racquet.

As a preliminary measure, Walker took Althea to a handball court and turned her loose with the racquet to hit the ball against the wall. Volleying with herself, she attacked the ball with speed and power. Walker kept Althea practicing on the handball court for several days to accustom her to wielding a regulation racquet, then he took her to a public tennis court where he arranged for a friend to go a few sets with her. Her play, remarkably good for the first attempt, amazed her opponent and those of the spectators aware that it was the girl's initial venture into tennis. Among them was a man who could appreciate what he was witnessing. An experienced player and member of the old Cosmopolitan Club—only a memory now but then a gathering place for black sports figures— he was so impressed that he took Althea to see Fred Johnson, the Cosmopolitan's one-armed tennis pro.

Johnson tried Althea on the court and he, too, was captivated by her obvious potential. Relying on his judgment, several club members undertook to pay for her lessons. Johnson began in earnest to work with her, trying to teach her how to smash out a service, to lob, to put top spin into a forehand and to undercut a backhand, to hammer overhead shots, and how to play a smart, strategically sound game. He tried to teach her footwork and network and control. A natural athlete, Althea had strength, endurance, and the will to win. She absorbed the coaching readily but resisted all efforts to alter her attitude. Still the cocky, street-hardened product of Harlem, she couldn't see why she should congratulate someone who beat her or why politely return a ball someone had clumsily let loose from a neighboring court.

One of the women members of the Cosmopolitan Club bought Althea her first tennis costume. Attired in the petite white outfit, Althea was grateful. She was, in fact, grateful for all that Walker, Johnson, and the members had done and were doing for her, but gratitude was a new emotion she did not quite know how to handle. The habits of independence, defiance, and suspicion were too ingrained.

Now fourteen, Althea no longer made a pretense of attending school. She had become a transient in her own home. For pocket money she found temporary, odd jobs—messenger, lunchroom helper, elevator operator. The only thing she did consistently was to practice tennis. Month by month her game improved. She did not learn to take the loss of a game gracefully but her losses became more and more rare.

In mid-1942, the club pro considered Althea ready for serious competition and entered her in the New York State Championships of the American Tennis Association, a black organization. She won her division. The club then entered her in the ATA girls' singles and she made it through the semifinals, but she was beaten in the finals. Chagrined by the loss, she practiced more fiercely than ever.

Because of the pressures of World War II, the ATA cancelled its major meets in 1943, but resumed the nationals the following year. Althea entered and captured the girls' singles national title, repeating the win in 1945. She turned eighteen in 1946 and moved up to the women's division of the ATA nationals. She was successful through the elimination rounds of the older division, but in the finals a more experienced player was too much for her. Glum over the defeat, Althea stalked off the court. She had no way of knowing that at that moment two spectators in the stands were starting to reshape her life.

Hubert A. Eaton and Robert W. Johnson were old friends who had a lot in common. Both were successful, black doctors in small Southern cities—Dr. Eaton in Wilmington, North Carolina, and Dr. Johnson in Lynchburg, Virginia—and both were enthusiastic, skilled tennis players. Now they had something else in common— recognition that the dejected girl walking off the court after her loss had played with a natural talent and drive that could lead her to greatness, given the proper help. The two doctors learned all they could about Althea and then went to her with an unusual, extremely generous proposition.

They proposed that she spend winters with the Eatons in Wilmington, attending the local high school and practicing tennis on Dr. Eaton's backyard court. She would spend summers in Lynchburg with the Johnsons, continuing her practice and traveling the ATA circuit with Dr. Johnson. The aim would be to put her in line for a college athletic scholarship, once high school was behind her, and to provide an avenue for realizing her full potential as a tennis player. As long as she kept her end of the bargain, both doctors would assume her support.

The offer stunned Althea; for once no quick retort came to her lips. She considered it from every angle, looking for booby traps, and could find none. Acceptance would mean abandoning old, impulsive ways and leading an orderly, conventional life. It would mean returning to the classroom with students younger than she. But it would also mean a comfortable home, good food, pocket money, and a chance to make a name for herself in tennis. She was confident she could develop the kind of tennis prowess envisioned for her, but she wondered if she could handle the rest of it. She decided to try.

Quiet Wilmington was strange after teeming Harlem, and the Eaton home was a mansion after the decaying tenements. The Eatons spoke, ate, dressed, conducted themselves differently from the ways she had known. For the first time in her life, Althea felt awkward and crude. She kept her eyes open, drinking everything in, trying to learn what this new environment was all about.

Althea took placement tests at Williston Industrial High and on the basis of them was placed in the sophomore class. She faced school with resignation and conquered the impulse to play hooky. She did something else that was a novelty for her—she studied. Between the rules and regulations of home life and school life, she felt chained, but the shackles began to feel lighter after a while.

Althea spent part of each day practicing tennis with Dr. Eaton, who was quite good, or with others—including some of Wilmington's better, white players—who gravitated to that hospitable backyard. Althea—now almost five-feet-eleven and a hard, lithe 145 pounds—played a strong, fast game, always out for a quick, overwhelming win. It was this compulsion to clobber her rivals that was her Achilles' heel; it made her impatient, sacrificing strategy to try for the quick kill. If she fell behind, she abandoned careful approaches and set-up shots and reverted to slam-bang play that usually only hastened defeat. Through that school year Dr. Eaton kept dinning it in to her: strategy, restraint, control. As summer approached he felt he was making some headway.

When school was out, Althea went to the Johnsons in Lynchburg. Dr. Johnson was pleased to see that her game had become more skillful, smarter, despite shortcomings that still emerged in the heat of play. There were off-the-court changes too. She had become more careful of her appearance and her manners, and had learned some of the social graces, although every once in a while traces of Harlem broke through.

Dr. Johnson and Althea started hitting the tournaments. Playing as a team, they won several mixed-doubles. As a solo entry, Althea won the women's singles in nine tournaments. The climax was to be the ATA nationals where she was favored to win the women's singles. She did not disappoint those who had predicted her victory, but the decisiveness of the win was more emphatic than many had expected: 6-3, 6-0. With the ATA title came recognition of Althea Gibson as the best black, woman tennis player in America.

After successfully defending her ATA crown in 1948, Althea was anxious to try her luck in the major league of tennis, tournaments sanctioned by the United States Lawn Tennis Association. But there was a stumbling block—the USLTA circuit was barred to blacks.

Working behind the scenes, several influential figures, both within the USLTA and the ATA, had joined forces to try to break the color bar. They had been seeking an outstanding black player with whom they could challenge the ban; they did not want to jeopardize their case with a player who might crack under the pressure. They thought Althea might be the person they sought.

Early in 1949 word filtered down to Althea through ATA channels that if she applied for entrance to the USLTA's Eastern Indoor Championships it would be considered favorably. She immediately fired off her entry form and when it was accepted she arranged for an excused absence from school. She acquitted herself reasonably well at the meet, hanging on until the quarterfinals. On the strength of that showing she was invited to play the following week in the National Indoor Championships. Again she made it to the quarterfinals where she was beaten by Nancy Chaffee, a fine performer. Althea's showing had been nothing to disdain, especially in light of the psychological burden she carried as a trailblazer for blacks. The progressives were satisfied that they had chosen well in selecting her to spearhead the drive to eliminate race from tennis.

Althea graduated from high school in June with an excellent academic record. She was awarded an athletic scholarship to Florida A.&M. in Tallahassee, and so at twenty-two she headed for college, the last place she would have expected to find herself back when she roamed the streets of Harlem.

At college she had a full load to carry—classes, tennis practice, playing on the basketball team, and working part-time as an assistant in the physical education department. It left little time for tournament play, though she did defend her ATA title successfully.

In 1950 Althea was again invited to enter the USLTA National Indoor meet and her play carried her all the way to the finals where her opponent was again Nancy Chaffee, her nemesis of the previous year. History repeated itself; Nancy beat her again. But if Althea had not demonstrated that she was the best in her tournament division, she had shown that she was second-best. This posed a major problem for white tennis because leading contenders rated bids to the Nationals in Forest Hills.

Never in the history of the most important tennis tournament in America had a black competed. Yet, Althea Gibson had clearly earned that right.

The crunch between justice and prejudice was too blatant to be swept under the rug. The press took up Althea's cause, dismissing as nonsense the contention of apologists that she had not proven herself in the major pre-Forest Hills, grass eliminations—Seabright, Orange, Essex, Hampton—nonsense because none of those private clubs permitted blacks on their courts.

Of all the editorials, the most telling was one by tennis-great Alice Marble in *American Lawn Tennis*. She deftly described how white tennis boxed Althea in by withholding invitations to the big Eastern grass meets and then penalizing her for not competing in them. "If Althea Gibson represents a challenge to the present crop of women players, it is only fair that they should meet the challenge on the courts, where tennis is played." Then, letting her anger show through, she went on, "If tennis is a game for ladies and gentlemen, it's also time we acted a little more like gentlepeople and less like sanctimonious hypocrites."

Althea was an island of apparent composure in the midst of the storm raging around her, recognizing that she could help her cause most by holding her tongue while the gentlepeople and the hypocrites squared off. Inwardly she churned with anxiety.

The die-hards caved in. Orange invited Althea to the Eastern Grass Courts Championship, a major stepping-stone to the Nationals. Although unaccustomed to grass, she beat her first-round opponently handily. She was eliminated in the second round, but in losing the battle she won the war—she had shown enough to make it unthinkable that she be denied admission to Forest Hills. Althea Gibson, out of a Silver cotton field via the streets of Harlem, had cracked the color bar in big-league tennis, just as Jackie Robinson had shattered racial barriers in big-league baseball three years earlier.

Nervous as a cat, Althea went to New York for the Nationals, staying with Mrs. Rhoda Smith, who had bought her her first tennis costume at the old Cosmopolitan Club nine years earlier. First-day play at Forest Hills was an ordeal for Althea, not on the court where she made short work of Barbara Knapp of England, 6-2, 6-2, but in the clubhouse where she was beseiged by the press.

Althea was given little chance of winning second-round play because her opponent was Louise Brough, earlier conqueror of both Forest Hills and Wimbledon. She was noticeably tense when she joined Louise on the court. Playing poorly, moving with a stiffness and hesitancy that were unlike her, Althea lost the first set, 6-1. In the second set she loosened up, her movements became faster, more fluid, more certain. She placed the ball well, stroking it powerfully, especially with her forehand. She won, 6-3. The third and final set was a stubborn duel. When the score went to 7-6 in Althea's favor she was only four shots away from victory and Louise was clearly tiring. The excited gallery recognized a stunning upset in the making. Then the sky suddenly darkened and a thunderstorm of tropical intensity broke out. Play was called and rescheduled for the next day.

The delay was costly to Althea, giving her too much time to think, to worry, to tense up. On the other hand, it gave her opponent a chance to recoup the strength that had been fading when the game had been called. When play resumed Althea showed sporadic flashes of her form of the day before but Louise was master of the court. Eliminated in three straight sets, Althea was utterly dejected.

On the way back to Tallahassee she replayed the match in her mind, trying to analyze her flaws so she could commence work to correct them. Of one thing she was certain: now that she had shattered the racial bars she would not abandon her drive to reach the top. She refused to be thwarted because she had the reactions of a fighter and because she realized she had become a symbol to blacks who counted on her to win for *them*.

Perhaps all the pressure made her try too hard. Whatever the reason, her game leveled off—good enough to stay in contention, not good enough to reach the pinnacle. She continued defending her ATA title successfully and winning regional tournaments, but victory in the most important meets eluded her.

In 1952 she was ranked No. 9 nationally. In 1953, when she graduated from college, she edged up to No. 7. That fall Althea became a physical education instructor at Lincoln University in Missouri. Thinking back on her former chronic truancy, she shook her head in wonder to find herself a member of a college faculty. As she must have asked herself, reverting to one of her favorite slang expressions, "Ain't that a blip?"

Despite her teaching responsibilities, Althea set aside time for long practice sessions and for tournament competition. But nothing changed—she could not forge to the front. When the 1954 rankings came out she had slipped to No. 12. It was all beginning to seem so futile. In early 1955, thoroughly discouraged, she made a decision that grieved her—when the academic year ended in June she would resign from the faculty and apply for a commission in the WAC, abandoning tennis.

Chance, which had played such a major role in her life, still had a twist or two left for Althea. Before she could join the WAC, the State Department asked her to make a tennis-playing good-will tour of the Far East with three other American players: Karol Fageros, Hamilton Richardson, and Bob Perry. She knew she was selected partly for her ability and partly because it would be a political plus for the U.S. to have a racially mixed foursome perform in Asia. She appreciated the wry irony of having her black skin work for her after having worked against her for so long.

The tour began in Burma, wound through India and Pakistan, and ended in Ceylon six weeks later. They were the most fateful six weeks of Althea's life. In that period she came fully of age, both as an individual and as a tennis player. Living cheek-by-jowl with each other, all four members of the team developed a close, deeply satisfying friendship that was color-blind on both sides. Off the court, they were swept up in a whirl of entertainment by the cream of local society. When conversation came around to America's racial problems, as it often did, Althea was the center of attention. The State Department had told her this would happen and had advised her to simply give her honest views, which she did with objectivity and dignity.

On the court, everything fell into place for Althea. At last she was doing all the right things at the right time and in the right way. She abandoned the continental grip in favor of the eastern, enabling her to achieve greater versatility in her forehand and backhand, and her wrist action was more limber than ever. She was doing so well that when the tour ended she remained in Europe for tournament competition before her hot streak could cool.

She played in Sweden, Germany, France, England, Italy, Egypt, winning meet after meet. Her sparkling performance earned her a bid to Wimbledon—tennis' closest approach to a world series.

On the way to England for Wimbledon play, Althea paused in Paris for the French Nationals. She was unbeatable through the elimination rounds and went into the finals against Angela Mortimer. Attacking relentlessly, Althea won the contest, 6-3 and 11-9, becoming the champion of France and the first black to win a truly major singles crown anywhere in the world. Althea was floating on air. Since leaving the U.S. eight months earlier she had entered 18 tournaments and had captured 16, 11 of them in a row.

Wimbledon brought Althea back to earth. Performing before the staid, hard-to-please gallery of 20,000, some of the bounce went out of her game. She had peaked at the French Nationals and now the strain of her months of barnstorming caught up with her. She did not force the game at the net with her usual ferocity, and a shade of strength was missing from her normally overpowering forehand. She made it to the quarterfinals where Shirley Fry beat her, 4-6, 6-3, 6-4.

In September, Althea played the U.S. Nationals at Forest Hills. She had recovered from the strain of her European tour and had regained her sharpness. She easily made it through the elimination rounds to the finals where her opponent was Shirley Fry, who had bested her at Wimbledon. Althea did not hold back at the net this time as she had in her last outing against Shirley, but now she went too far in the other direction, rushing the net so fast that errors crept into her game. Shirley played a steady, calculated game, especially effective along the baseline, and beat Althea in two sets, 6-3, 6-4. Later, when Althea could reflect calmly on the year now drawing to a close, she realized that 1956 had been her turning point. She had won several major tournaments and had built a solid international reputation. The two big ones, Wimbledon and Forest Hills, would not forever elude her; she was confident of that.

Althea planned 1957 carefully, confining competition to grass events because she was priming herself for Wimbledon and Forest Hills, both of them played on grass. She did not defend her French title because she did not want to slacken her pace on the slow, composition courts of Paris' Roland Garros Stadium. The tournaments she did enter she won, and won well. Between meets she worked out under the critical eye of Sydney Llewellyn, an astute coach.

When the 1957 rankings came out, Althea had moved up to No. 2. In July, when it was Wimbledon time again, she was ready for the big test.

An almost unprecedented heat wave gripped England during Wimbledon Week and the stadium was an oven. The shirt-sleeved throng in the stands was a sea of fluttering programs pressed into service as fans. Althea blocked all distractions from her mind, conscious of nothing except the court and the opponent. She played consistent, confident, smart tennis, tempering her strength and speed with strategy, not trying to kill every ball, not plunging impetuously toward the net when wisdom dictated laying back. Her patient, skillful play carried her through the elimination rounds with surprising ease. Now only one hurdle remained between her and the Wimbledon crown—Darlene Hard of California, the other finalist.

Excitement gripped the baking stadium for the pay-off round. Precisely at 1:15 Althea and Darlene took their places on the center court. Althea won the toss and elected to serve. Her first service was a powerful, booming, well-placed shot, a harbinger of things to come. She was superb, lightning-fast, sustained, masterful both at the net and in the backcourt. Her game had the strength of a man and the elegance of a woman. She captured the first set, 6-3.

In the second set Althea maintained her controlled, attacking game. Weakening under the constant pressure, Darlene began committing costly errors. Althea brought in a 6-2 victory and with it she conquered Wimbledon. A few minutes later, standing on the turf where other tennis immortals had stood before her, Althea Gibson accepted from Queen Elizabeth the gold salver emblematic of the Wimbledon title. It was a soul-stirring moment for her.

That evening at the Wimbledon Ball, Althea made the traditional victory speech, saying in part, "I am humbly grateful and deeply aware of the responsibility involved in the wearing of this crown. God grant that I wear it with dignity, defend it with honor, and, when my day is done, relinquish it gracefully." Those words, such a just-right blend of pride and humility, revealed how thoroughly the sullenly rebellious urchin of another era had been transformed.

In September she played in the U.S. Nationals in Forest Hills. From the start she looked like a winner. It was Wimbledon all over again—she was unbeatable, reaching the finals without the loss of a set. By a curious quirk, the other finalist was Louise Brough, who had eliminated Althea in her initial Forest Hills appearance in 1950.

Play began on a cautious note, each probing for weaknesses to exploit. As they got the measure of each other the contest opened up into a fast, hard duel. The set ended in Althea's favor, 6-3.

Having failed to shake her opponent, Louise Brough's confidence began to crack in the second set. She tried to speed up her serves, only to make deadly double-faults. She hammered at Althea's backhand, hoping to weaken it, only to see that backhand grow even stronger. Althea sparkled, playing with pinpoint accuracy and verve. She defeated her rival, 6-2, to win the set and the United States title. When she was presented the championship trophy, she drew the greatest ovation ever heard in that stadium.

It had been a long, discouragingly difficult climb upward from the cottonfields in Silver, along the alleys of Harlem, over the color bar, through the years of tournament reverses. Now Althea Gibson had finally reached the summit—she had conquered Wimbledon and Forest Hills. She had persevered to become the world's foremost woman tennis player.

To revert to the original Gibsonese, "Ain't it a blip?"

5   The Man Who
Rolled Back Clouds

Glenn Cunningham

IT WAS MIDWINTER, 1916, and for seven-year-old
Glenn and his brother, Floyd, the day began like any
other. As usual, they were the first to arrive at school.
Following their regular routine, they set about building a
fire in the pot-bellied stove to knock the chill from the air
for the later arrivals.

Floyd shook down the ashes; Glenn brought in kin-
dling and coal. If either had known that the Ladies' Liter-
ary Society had met in the school the previous evening
they might have been more cautious. As it was, neither
discovered the glowing coals hidden among the ashes nor
the gasoline for the ladies' lanterns now in the can normally containing kerosene to prime the stove.

Floyd tilted the can; the fluid trickled down, reaching
the live coals. The resulting explosion enveloped the boys
in a ball of flame. Somehow, they made it back to their
farm home.

Both boys were frightening apparitions—singed and
blackened, a sickening odor of charred flesh clinging to
them. Their horrified parents carried them to their beds

and called the doctor, pleading with him to hurry.

After working over the boys for hours, the doctor sadly told the hovering parents, "I wish I could hold out hope for Floyd. At least Glenn will live, although he may never walk again."

After Floyd's funeral the doctor returned to change Glenn's dressings; already he had been forced to remove a small portion of the left foot and he prayed no further amputation would be necessary. The dressings changed, he patted Glenn on the shoulder and said, "When the weather turns warm we'll get you into a chair out on the porch."

Glenn looked up at the doctor. "I don't want to sit. I want to walk and run. And I will. I will." There was no doubt in his voice. The doctor turned away.

After four painful months, scar tissue covered the wounds but the legs remained useless, skin taut, tendons unresponsive, muscles tight, twisted, powerless. But Glenn remained convinced that those legs would again jump and skip and run as he might command them. His mother, too wise to ignore the power of a child's belief, began a daily ritual of kneading the damaged muscles and flexing the legs. When fatigue forced her to halt, Glenn took over, reaching down to massage until his fingers ached.

Six months after the accident the doctor was transfixed by the sight of the boy walking. It was a strange gait—a slow, sidewise limp—but for all that, Glenn was walking unaided. The boy laughed at the doctor's surprise. "But I told you I'd walk," he said with the irrefutable logic of the young. "Next time I'll run."

Two years after the fire the doctor did behold the wonderful sight of Glenn running, not fast, but running. Now he ran everywhere for the sheer joy of it. Slowly, speed and strength and even grace came to those restless legs, and only if one knew what to look for could the lingering suggestion of a limp be detected.

When Glenn was eleven his eye was captured by a magnificent display in a shop window. Gleaming like jewels was an array of medals to be awarded in schoolboy races scheduled for that afternoon. Glenn was torn between the beauty of the medals and the knowledge that he was expected home promptly. Beauty won—he headed for the athletic field.

Glenn entered the mile race and as he waited for earlier events to be held, he reached down from habit to massage his legs. At last he lined up with the others and when the starting gun cracked, he was off as though catapulted. Glenn was suffused with rapture—he was running, running, running. The boy who might never have walked won the race. The sweetest sound he ever heard was the judge calling, "First place, Glenn Cunningham!"

In high school he continued to compete and to win, but now the joy he derived from it assumed a new dimension. From his searing accident and his triumph over it came a conviction that all children, given determination and motivation and a chance, can overcome the gravest handicaps to achieve success. Groping for meaning in his own experience, he decided that he was meant to pass on to others the lesson he had learned. His ordeal by fire shaped his future: he would devote himself to encouraging young people to realize their full potential. First, though, he had his own education to complete before he could guide others.

Knowing his family could not afford college expenses, Cunningham set about earning the money himself. At every opportunity he worked at odd jobs for farmers in the area and his bankbook began to show reassuring entries. "I was tightfisted, saving 99 cents of every dollar I earned," he recalls with a smile. His memory is a bit faulty—he was thrifty but not tightfisted. When the 1929 Depression struck, he withdrew his savings to lend to the very farmers from whom he earned the money. He entered college with a zero bank balance, but "it did not matter. I worked my way through and the economies I had to practice were good training."

By allocating time carefully, Glenn was able to join the track team. He had developed into a powerful distance runner, with endurance for the long haul and enough in reserve for a burst at the finish. The coaches built on that solid base, adding the polish and refinement to make him a formidable competitor. He won with regularity and soon intercollegiate records were falling beneath his driving legs. The track world began taking notice of Glenn Cunningham. It was no surprise to the experts when he was granted a berth on the U.S. team in the 1932 Olympics in Los Angeles.

Cunningham was entered in the 1,500-meter event, a distance that had become his specialty. He tried to quell his nervousness as he waited for the race to get under way. When the gun sounded he made a good, clean start and he poured it on, giving it everything he had. He pulled into the lead and maintained it most of the distance but his tremendous effort cost him—he did not have enough left for a strong kick at the finish. He came in fourth. Though he was disappointed, those who knew he was running with a piece of one foot missing hailed his performance as a near-miracle. The following year he received the James Sullivan Award as the nation's outstanding amateur athlete.

Cunningham was granted his bachelor's degree in 1934 and his master's in 1936. He had never weakened in his resolve to try to reach the minds of the young. To give himself the most effective preparation for that effort he immediately began work on his doctorate in education. But he did not turn his back on the track. He continued to practice and to compete as he undertook his advanced studies. The 1936 Olympics were rapidly approaching and he hoped to be a part of the U.S. team in Berlin.

He made the team and again he would be competing in the 1,500-meter event. He went to Berlin with high hopes. But soon after the team arrived and scant days before Cunningham was to run, his old leg troubles flared up so painfully that each practice was a painful ordeal. The team doctors worked frantically on those scarred legs but they feared that he would be sidelined. They had made the same error as the country doctor in Kansas in 1916—they had looked at the legs and not at the whole man. Not only did he compete, he broke the 1932 record set in the Los Angeles Olympics. But the phenomenal John Lovelock of New Zealand also broke the old mark and he nosed Cunningham out for the gold medal. Cunningham had to content himself with the second-place silver.

Running had become a part of Glenn Cunningham's life and he continued competing after returning to the campus to resume work on his doctorate. As he had done as a young schoolboy, he still ran for the sheer joy of it. If he broke records in the process so much the better—but being able to run was the main thing. His joy in pounding around the track seemed to lend wings to his feet—he was performing better than ever. In 1938, invited to a meet at Dartmouth College, he ran the indoor paced mile in 4:04.4—then the world's fastest time either indoors or out. The miracle had come to pass—the boy who was not supposed to walk had become the fastest miler anywhere.

There was another significant moment for Cunningham in 1938; he was granted his doctorate. His long preparation for service to youth completed, he became director of physical education at Cornell College in Iowa where he devised an improved student health program that became a model for many other schools.

Cunningham believes in the Biblical injunction to "cast thy bread upon the waters." With the country emerging from the Depression, every farmer to whom he had earlier lent his savings now repaid him. "The timing was perfect," he says. "Earning a regular salary, I had no need for the money so I made fortunate investments that turned out to be quite profitable."

In 1946, after wartime Navy service, Glenn sat down with his wife, Ruth, to consider their future. He had seen the misery of war and always, it seemed to him, it was the children who were the most defenseless victims. He knew he would not be content to return to the well-ordered routine of a college campus; for him, the real need was to help unfortunate youngsters to whom a college campus might seem an unobtainable dream. It was providential that Ruth shared his vision. Now the true significance of his profitable investments became apparent, for they provided the independence to permit his undertaking.

Returning to Kansas, the couple bought a beautiful, 849-acre ranch. Then Glenn went forth in aid of disadvantaged youth. Ranging the entire country, he visited schools, churches, youth groups, civic clubs, to preach better education, greater spiritual and moral values, perseverance in the face of reverses, human kindness. His adult audiences were stirred by his message and its undeniable truths. His young audiences were inspired by this visible proof that heroes are made, not born, that despite unfavorable odds the individual has within himself the capacity to succeed.

After an address to a church group in late 1946, the minister called him aside. "There is a boy here in desperate need of help," he said. "Billy is apathetic, completely wrapped in a shell that nobody can pierce and it is warping him. The sad fact is that his parents simply have no feeling for him. They have five older children and Billy was an unwelcome addition. They resent this unwanted mouth to feed and they let Billy know it. I've tried and failed to find a way out of the dilemma. Can you help?"

Cunningham returned home with Billy in tow. The Cunninghams nourished him with love as well as food, let him know in a hundred ways that he was wanted and cherished. "I finally cracked Billy's protective armor when I took him to the corral one day," Cunningham recalls with obvious satisfaction. "I could see that those beautiful horses excited him. 'Pick the one you want,' I told him. 'He's yours for as long as you are here and nobody will touch him without your permission. But he will depend on you alone; if you don't feed, water, and care for him nobody else will.' "

That was the first time that anything of consequence

had belonged to Billy, the first living thing to depend on him for its well-being. The horse turned out to be the perfect medicine to cure Billy's man-made illness. Today he is a successful, outgoing rancher with a corral full of handsome horses.

Billy was the first in what would become the ranch's most flourishing crop. Others learned about the youngster and many had a Billy or a Susan of their own for the Cunninghams to nourish. Urgent letters and phone calls came from California, Indiana, Georgia, from everywhere. We have a boy who has been abandoned . . . whose parents abuse him . . . a girl whose mother is a prostitute . . . will you help? So much misery and young suffering, so much final catastrophe to be averted.

Neither of the Cunninghams could refuse a plea for help. Since 1946, churches, civic groups, social workers, and juvenile authorities have referred well over 8,000 children to them. Some have stayed weeks, some years. As with the original Billy, each arrival picks a horse as his very own. So convinced is Cunningham of the efficacy of "animal therapy" that the horses were augmented by a miniature zoo that includes elk, buffalo, reindeer, and typical barnyard animals. The four-footed "therapists," like their two-footed "patients," receive large doses of love. Clearly, this ranch is not run like a boot camp, but it is not without its discipline.

Cunningham believes in the "spare-the-rod-and-spoil-the-child" concept, insisting the rod be applied fairly and promptly. However, he firmly opposes tongue-lashings. He illustrates his reason with Steve whose father had confessed, "The boy defeats me. Every time he got in trouble I'd bawl him out and he'd just get meaner. No matter how much I cussed him out it did no good. Maybe you can do something with him; I can't."

The first time Steve acted up after he got to the ranch, Cunningham upended him for a no-nonsense spanking. When it was over, Steve fled to the pasture. Later he returned and told Cunningham, "You didn't yell or cuss. You got mad because I did something wrong and you cared enough to give me the licking I had coming. I really matter to you, don't I?"

The truth is that all children matter deeply to the Cunninghams. They open their arms and hearts to children, counsel them, inspire them, give them goals and the hope of reaching them, teach them to live with others in harmony and mutual respect, nourish their bodies and minds. But the Cunninghams never coddle; to each they allot a fair share of duties and responsibilities that must be discharged. Foremost is school and diligent effort to become a proficient student. Other duties include helping in the fields and ranch buildings, raking, cleaning, cooking, mending, painting, canning; the list is long and varied. Whatever the task, the child is taught to do it wholeheartedly as his contribution to the common good.

Realistic about his wards, Cunningham recognizes their limitations, sets attainable goals, and then insists on utmost effort to achieve those goals. At the county school the children attend, Joe—one of the slowest learners ever at the ranch—had been placed in a special class for poor students, a class many of his schoolmates called the "nut hatch." Cunningham knew Joe was no Phi Beta Kappa but he also knew he was no "nut." Working patiently with the boy, Cunningham gradually infused him with a will to learn, to stretch his mind, to open his books with determination and even pleasure. The first time Joe brought home a "C," Cunningham crowed proudly, and there was no holding him when Joe got his first "B." "He became a solid, average student and that was complete success because he was realizing his full potential," Cunningham says. "There is no stigma in being average, only in being below average when you have the capacity to rise to the middle."

The ranch could produce most of the children's food but it could not grow their shoes, clothes, schoolbooks, hair ribbons, medicines. Cunningham's funds, once so substantial, dwindled. They were forced to sell the ranch and move to a smaller one. But, pinched for money or not, they continued to tell the pastor or social worker or juvenile authority who telephoned, "Of course the child can stay with us for as long as necessary to work out the problem."

The cardinal principle governing Glenn Cunningham is that a young life is not a commodity to be discussed in terms of expense, that the miseries, bewilderment and problems of youth cannot be handled like marketplace transactions. "Every child must have his chance to become a useful, happy, well-adjusted adult," he says firmly. "He must not be denied the counsel, encouragement, and honest, unselfish love he deserves. No child is basically bad—only environments and adult examples are bad. Change them and the goodness in the child shines through."

And so Dr. Glenn Cunningham, the champion runner who was not expected to walk, challenged the clouds blighting young lives, rolling them back to let youthful goodness shine through.

6 Indestructible Is the Name for Him

Jerry Kramer

GREEN BAY, WISCONSIN, takes its football seriously. Elsewhere it might be merely a pastime but in Green Bay it is a cult and its priesthood is the Packers of the National Football League. And of all the Packers, one occupies a place of special affection in Green Bay. It is partly because No. 64—Jerry Kramer—was so prodigal in working gridiron miracles and partly because, like Lazarus, he came back from the dead. At least, from the near-dead.

On a December day in 1964, a report that the big guard had just died on a hospital operating table stunned all Green Bay. Within minutes, newspaper, television, and radio switchboards were swamped with calls. Countless grieving citizens telephoned the Kramer home to offer condolences. In Kramer's favorite barber shop the disconsolate regulars chipped in for a tremendous floral offering. The anguish gripping Green Bay was premature—Kramer had been an eyelash away from death but had fought back from the brink once again.

To dispel the gloom, United Press International had to flash a story over its wires denying that the football great

82

was dead. A short time later, Kramer himself—haggard and weak but with a sense of humor intact—hosted a mock wake, complete with enough beer to wash away all traces of mourning.

Jerry Kramer was only five when he first demonstrated his ability to stave off death. Firewood had to be chopped at the family farm in Idaho and Jerry knew that his father and older brother were working in the fields and his mother was busy in the kitchen. He had often seen how the others wielded the big, double-bitted ax, so he went to the woodshed to handle the chore himself. Setting a limb in place against the block, he raised the heavy ax over his head. Somehow the implement slipped from his grasp and plummeted down, the razor-keen blade slashing his chin and neck. Blood spurted in a crimson stream. Aghast, Mrs. Kramer stanched the flow as best she could and rushed him to the hospital. Had the wounds been a fraction deeper, the doctors would have been unable to save him.

The near-fatal accident scarcely slowed Jerry Kramer down. A five-year-old usually heals fast and forgets even faster; before the stitches were out Jerry was scampering about again.

By the time he entered high school Kramer had discovered an organized outlet for his energy—team athletics. He liked all sports but he was really in his natural element on the gridiron. He had developed a linesman's build—thick, muscular thighs, barrel-like chest, broad shoulders and strong arms—and had sure, quick moves. He thrived on the constant pressure and jarring contact of the game and had no trouble making tackle on the freshman team.

Even then one could discern an emerging aggressive, hard-charging, head-on pattern to his play. Football is notorious for hobbling its players with injuries and those with Kramer's style are especially vulnerable; yet, his only injury that season came in the manual arts class when he inadvertently backed into a lathe that tore a gobbet of flesh from his hip.

The next year Kramer—taller, heavier, more experienced—was a varsity starter. He also began throwing the discus and putting the shot with the track team. He made it all the way to mid-November without an injury.

A few days before Thanksgiving, Kramer and some friends went bird hunting. Although Jerry knew proper gun-handling, somehow his shotgun discharged, shooting him in the right arm and side. For an instant he stared in astonishment at his mangled flesh, then he ran to a nearby farmhouse. The farmer scorched the road to the hospital.

The doctors quickly tied off blood vessels and cleaned the wounds of debris so they could judge the extent of damage. What they found worried them—much of the right forearm muscle had been destroyed, both major bones below the elbow were fractured, a wrist nerve was crushed, and three pellets had punctured the liver. On top of all that, Kramer had lost a vast quantity of blood and his pulse had become feeble.

From the moment—hours later—that their patient was wheeled from surgery, the medical staff maintained a constant vigil, keeping him sedated against pain and dosed with antibiotics to combat infection. It was four days before they could rate him a better than even chance to pull through, but they feared they would have to amputate the arm. The mutilated flesh had developed an ominous, spreading red blotch. It was another three days before Kramer's name could be removed from the critical list, but it was still doubtful that the arm could be saved. Then the matter resolved itself when the arm suddenly responded to medication and showed signs of healing.

With amputation eliminated, a series of delicate operations were undertaken to recapture as much as possible of the natural movement and appearance of the arm, but plastic surgery and other procedures could accomplish just so much. After the final operation, the limb was scarred and rutted like a field prepared for spring planting and two fingers were bent almost like a longshoreman's baling hook. Kramer was so relieved simply to have the arm that he shrugged off its appearance.

While still hospitalized, he embarked on a strenuous routine of exercise to restore strength and mobility to the arm. Five months after the harrowing accident he competed in a track and field meet. He put the shot splendidly with that patched-together arm of his. One heave—just two inches shy of 52 feet—set a new, state-wide, scholastic record.

That summer disaster struck again in the kind of extraordinary accident that had become Jerry Kramer's dubious trademark. Returning home one afternoon, he spotted a calf frisking loose in the field. Taking off in pursuit, he tried to head it back to the barn. As he finally closed in on the elusive calf, it made a spinning leap to escape. One of its hooves crashed down on a brittle, weathered board, splitting it into jagged fragments that lanced upward. One large fragment pierced Kramer's groin. Almost by reflex, he pulled it free. Then there was another rush trip to the hospital where, by now, he was a familiar face.

The doctors cleaned the deep wound and probed for residue, finding none. The next day Kramer was seized by acute pain in his abdomen. The local hospital sent him to a better-equipped facility in Spokane where a 7-inch sliver of wood was found lodged against his spine. Had it gone undetected a few days longer it almost surely would have pierced the spine.

When Kramer graduated from high school he did it with a bang that made both the sports and the news pages. The sports columns reported that he had been selected for All-State football honors and had accepted an athletic scholarship to the University of Idaho. The news columns detailed his latest accident, a spectacular car wreck. He and a friend had been driving along a country road; the friend was at the wheel. In Jerry's words, "He got going a little fast—it must have been near a hundred miles an hour—when he lost control and the car went off the road." Remarkably, neither of the two youths was seriously hurt.

It was on the Idaho team that Kramer really came into his own. One of Kramer's athletic assets was his coachability and in this he was fortunate because Skip Stahley, coach of the Idaho Vikings, really knew his football and his players and had a fine talent for putting the two together adroitly. Stahley experimented with Kramer at guard and drilled him in the necessary adjustments for a successful transition from tackle. Stahley also used him to kick conversions, and he exhibited accuracy in lofting the ball between the uprights.

Kramer managed to stay clear of accidents until his

third year at Idaho and then he sustained a neck injury in a pile-up on the field. X-ray revealed a chipped vertebra. After corrective surgery he had a six-inch, crisscross scar running down from his collar bone. His body, stitched fore and aft, was starting to look as though it had been put together at a ladies' quilting bee.

There is sometimes a tendency to feel that football players must be treated gently in academic situations to avoid undue strain on the intellectual apparatus with which some consider them to be meagerly equipped. Kramer demonstrated that he was no college "jock," fit only for snap courses taught by lenient professors. In the classroom he displayed acumen and mental aplomb that needed no pampering. He was that rare campus bird who can soar with the Saturday afternoon heroes and peck with the midweek "brains."

Kramer also revealed that he could flap his wings with the college pranksters. In one nighttime lark, he climbed to a third-floor, frat house balcony to toll a large bell hung there to be pealed on special occasions. Grasping the rope, he pulled energetically, sending brazen tones ringing out over the startled campus. Then he turned to beat a hasty retreat. Apparently the balcony had not been designed for a 235-pound bell-ringer—it collapsed under him. In the instant he felt it giving way, Kramer lunged upward, grasping the eaves and dangling there sheepishly until rescuers hauled him through a window. The Class of '58 still speak in awe of the time he pealed the bell and peeled the balcony.

In his last year at Idaho, Kramer was a gridiron stalwart. Skip Stahley hailed him as one of the best guards he'd ever seen anywhere, either on offense or defense.

He closed out his college career by playing the East-West Shrine Game and then the North-South Senior Bowl, the first Idaho player ever selected for the latter game. It was a foregone conclusion that the pros would claim Kramer; it was only a question of which team would get to him first. Speculation was put to rest when the Green Bay Packers drafted him.

The Packers of 1958, in the midst of a massive rebuilding program to regain the greatness of earlier years, were not an easy team to break in with. The pressure on every player was intense because each knew he was readily expendable unless he demonstrated that he could contribute significantly and quickly in the search for a formula for success. Everyone was straining for performance that year and Jerry Kramer strained along with them.

The Packers began to jell in 1959 under the new coach, Vince Lombardi, an innovative, demanding perfectionist who drove his players hard and struck sparks in them. He hammered on fundamentals, taking nothing for granted. He introduced intricate running plays, making them a major part of Packer strategy, and knocked heads together until the team had them down pat. Prior to each game he schooled his men in the opposition's brand of play so that each man knew exactly what to expect from his opposite number and how to meet it effectively. And he forced his team to think and act like winners. His formula worked—the Packers were breaking out of the doldrums.

Kramer, in the offensive guard slot, had never worked harder. He was developing new skill and adroitness in leading running plays through the defending linemen, barreling in to make his man commit himself so the back

Barney Ross in 1933, the lightweight champion of the world

Ben Hogan, one of the finest all-time competitive golfers

Glenn Cunningham in the mile run at the Penn Relays, 1934

Tenley Albright at a practice session in Vienna in 1955

UPI Photo

Carole Heiss, Olympic gold medalist in 1960

UPI Photo

Alonzo Wilkins, President of the Eastern Wheelchair Basketball Conference

Pete Gray, left fielder with the St. Louis Browns, during a
game with the Yankees, at Yankee Stadium, 1945

Babe Didrikson, winner of the javelin throw and the hurdle
events of the 1932 Olympics

Paul Berlenbach (left) and Young Stribling at the New York
Velodrome

Jerry Kramer, offensive right guard of the Green Bay Packers

Sammy Lee, Olympic diving champion—twice

Althea Gibson, defending her title at Wimbledon in 1958

Jim Hurtubise in 1965 after his successful comeback to racing

Gordie Howe (9) passes the puck to his son Mark (5) just
before his 50th birthday

Kramer was leading could slant off in the opposite direction. If his man tried to meet him head-on and low, Kramer drove just as low, crashing in helmet to helmet. He was exhausted after each game, his nose red and raw where the helmet had been smashed down by the furious blocks, but his spirits soared because he knew he was playing good ball.

The rebuilding of the Packers came to flower in 1960. That year they had the touch of the great Green Bay teams of the past. And Kramer had earned the right to be part of the star-studded team because he was recognized as almost a casebook example of what a classic guard is all about; his straight-ahead blocks, his lead-out of the running backs, his agility in providing leak-proof pass protection, were gems. He and Fuzzy Thurston, Packer left guard, were hailed as the "Fearsome Twosome," the wiliest practitioners of their bruising art on any gridiron.

With his remarkable history as the pronest of the accident-prone, and with his fierce pace in a sport noted for injuries, Kramer was a prime candidate for disaster. Oddly, his hurts from the time Green Bay drafted him until midway in 1960 were only run-of-the-mill aches, sprains, and bruises as common to football as numbers on the jerseys. Then on November 20, in a game against the Los Angeles Rams, Kramer ran into a problem that could not be solved by tape, diathermy, or even Novocain.

It was an earmuff kind of day. As always when the mercury drops, there was a nagging ache in the permanently hooked fingers of Kramer's right hand, but he had long ago learned to ignore it. Halfway into the game he put a crashing block on L.A.'s Lamar Lundy and both giants hit the ground. Gasping for breath, Kramer climbed to his feet groggily and remained groggy for the balance of the game. Later, lingering under the shower, the water seemed to wash away the body aches but his head remained fogged.

In the days that followed, recurring lights flashed before Kramer's eyes, momentarily blotting out his vision. He played in five succeeding games, still handicapped by impaired vision. In December the Packers won the Western Conference and were slated to meet the Eagles, Eastern winners, for the NFL crown.

On the day of the big game Kramer's eyes were bothering him acutely but he said nothing about it because he was determined to be in on the Packer bid for the crown. It was a close game and the Eagles took it in a squeaker, 17-13. After the shouting was over and the season was behind him, Kramer turned himself in to the team doctor who found that he had been playing for over a month with a torn retina. The guard checked into the hospital for delicate corrective surgery.

When the bandages were removed, Kramer swivelled his gaze around the room to test his vision. A smile creased his ruggedly handsome face—the flashing lights had disappeared. He had something besides the repaired eye to comfort him—he had just been named an All-Pro.

When the '61 season opened, disaster struck Kramer early. Nailed on a defensive trap in a game against Minnesota, he ended up under more than a half-ton of the Viking forward wall. There was a sharp, shocking pain as a bone in his leg snapped under its load. It was a severe break of the tibia complicated by separation of the bone from its ankle socket. Kramer was laid out on an operat-

ing table for the umpteenth time. An orthopedic specialist pegged the bone to the ankle with a steel pin, confident that in time his patient would return to normal
activity, but he was less confident about a return to the
abnormality of football. But the guard had no doubts—
he *knew* he'd be back.

There were skeptics when Kramer checked in at the
1962 Packer training camp for the annual, preseason torture session but when they saw him perform on the field
they relaxed. He was as good as ever, as agile, strong, and
aggressive. He had exercised his leg faithfully since the
operation, it had responded well, and that was that.

Halfway through the schedule, Paul Hornung was injured and the brilliant halfback was to be sidelined for
the remaining games. There was sufficient bench depth
to replace him at halfback but Hornung was also place
kicker and there was no bench depth in kickers. Lombardi handed the kicking responsibility to Kramer, which
was asking a lot of a man who had done no serious place-
ments since college. But, with Starr holding for him, the
guard exuded confidence. His kicks were no things of
beauty—unorthodox, end-over-enders—but he was accurate and that was what counted. Between his brilliant play
on the line and his effective kicking, the guard was a key
sparkplug of the '62 Packers. He ran up a cumulative
total of 65 points in field goals and PATs, and by the time
December 30 rolled around the Packers were in Yankee
Stadium facing the New York Giants for the NFL title.

It required dedication for a fan to show up that
day—at game time it was 17 degrees with wind gusts of
30 miles per hour. The hooked fingers of Kramer's right
hand throbbed but he had his mind on other things as

the two teams lined up. And once the game got under way the 62,000 fans who had braved the weather had their hardihood suitably rewarded. They witnessed a gem, an exciting game and a personal triumph for Jerry Kramer.

Five minutes into the first period, Kramer kicked a field goal from the 26, bringing the game's first score. In the second period, Taylor went over for a touchdown from seven yards out. Kramer kicked the PAT, making it a 10-0 game. After the half-time break, the Giants got on the board with a blocked-punt recovery in the Packer end zone. The extra point was good, bringing the score to 10-7. All the rest of the scoring belonged to Jerry Kramer. In the third period he kicked a field goal from the 29; in the fourth he repeated from the 30. The game ended in a 16-7 victory and an NFL championship for the Packers. Kramer made All-Pro once again.

After that great season, '63 was a letdown for Green Bay. Hornung was lost for the year, this time not through injury but through discovery that he had been placing game bets. The tainted affair and the hole he left in the squad took something out of the players; they could not reach the peak of the prior year. Only Kramer, again kicking for the absent Hornung, was in consistently top form. He kicked for a season total of 91 points, a new Green Bay record.

The following year there was optimism in the Packer training camp. Hornung had been returned to the active roster and the team looked sharp in scrimmage. But for Kramer, there was a cloud on the horizon. He experienced constant fatigue, had lost his appetite, and was underweight. When the Packers broke camp he was running a temperature and was bothered by stomach and chest pains.

Dosed with pain-killer, Kramer played in the first two games of the new season. Then he discovered a lump low in his chest. It rapidly ballooned to the dimensions of a grapefruit and all Kramer could think of was *cancer*. He checked in to St. Vincent's in Green Bay for exploratory surgery.

When the surgical team laid bare the tumor they were deeply disturbed by its appearance. A hard mass lodged between liver and diaphragm, it was grossly infected. Dr. Robert G. Brault, the chief surgeon, removed a sample and rushed it to the lab for pathological analysis. The report, ruling out cancer, pinpointed the trouble as actinomycosis, a disease rare in humans but common in cattle. Amazingly, it was a delayed kick from the farmyard calf of so long ago. The germs driven into Kramer on the lancing fragment of board had been lurking in his body for twelve years. Dr. Brault removed the infected mass and closed the incision.

Early in October Kramer was released from St. Vincent's, weak and woefully underweight but radiating confidence. He even spoke of rejoining the team before the season ended. Then, abruptly, his temperature shot up and a second lump developed in his chest. A fresh round of surgery revealed deep-seated infection and a quantity of unhealed tissue but no cancer. After the operation Kramer developed pneumonia. To aggravate matters, he was in constant pain and the incision refused to knit together. His weight continued to drop.

Once again the surgeons cut open that tortured body but found no infected matter within and so closed the incision. Lying in his hospital bed, Kramer did a lot of thinking. He knew his system could not stand much more abuse and, as he expressed it, "I made peace with myself. I realized I'd been around 28 years and had a great life. Compared to people who never had anything, I had no gripe. If I had to go, I had to go."

Weeks later, feeble and in pain and 50 pounds underweight, Kramer persuaded his doctors to let him return home for Christmas. It was at this time that reports of his death were sweeping through Green Bay. Arriving in town looking like a ghost but obviously alive, he laid the rumors to rest.

Spring arrived and he was still suffering persistent pain, weakness, and fever, and the last of his many incisions had not yet healed. Dr. Brault decided that there would have to be still another operation. In May, Kramer—by now a medical curiosity—returned to St. Vincent's and a team of surgeons went to work on him. For almost seven hours they cut and probed. At last they discovered the source of his troubles—three small fragments of wood that had punctured his intestine. The slivers, slowly releasing bacteria, had gone undetected in his body for twelve years, masked by the vast quantity of internal scar tissue and the general disarray of his patched-together organs.

With the elusive root of his illness finally ferreted out and eliminated, Kramer experienced a sensation almost of rebirth. He could feel his body taking hold, now that it was at last rid of the burden it had carried for so long. His temperature became normal, his appetite returned, and the pain disappeared.

Kramer's buoyant spirits were not disturbed by two

further corrective operations the doctors ordered—he
knew that the worst was behind him. The last of the
operations, a hernia repair, was the eighth he had en-
dured in less than twelve months. Just before undergoing
it in June he predicted that he would be back in the
Green Bay lineup that year.

Few believed the guard's prediction of a return to the
gridiron so soon. Coach Lombardi did not expect Kramer
to make his comeback until the '66 season if, indeed,
there would be any comeback at all. Yet, when the 1965
training camp opened there was Jerry Kramer ready to
suit up. His surgical marathon had left him 25 pounds
too light and his old bounce was not yet back. When he
stripped in the locker room, there on display was the evidence of what he had been through—the network of
scars, some old, some new, tic-tac-toeing his entire torso.
But one thing the scalpels had not tampered with was his
grit—that was intact.

Acutely aware of Kramer's long ordeal, the coaches
treated him like a hothouse flower, letting him practice
kicking but keeping him out of scrimmages. Kramer had
other ideas. He did his kicking as directed and then after
each day's session ended he remained behind to work out
on his own—throwing blocks against the dummy, doing
calisthenics, grinding away the rust that had accumulated
during his long layoff. He was weary when he tumbled
into bed each night but it was a satisfying weariness because he knew he was making progress. He was becoming
stronger, faster, more nimble. His weight was creeping
up to normal and his endurance was returning. He had
risen from the near-dead and was now vibrantly alive.

The first preseason game was to be an exhibition

against the New York Giants and Kramer was determined to be there in his old slot at offensive right guard. Several days before the game he commenced badgering Lombardi but the coach was reluctant to throw Kramer to the wolves so soon. The guard was obstinate and persuasive. Lombardi caved in, not without misgivings.

The game was played in Green Bay. When Kramer took his place in the lineup, a thunderous ovation ripped from the crowded stands; protracted and insistent, it drowned out the PA announcements. It was a thrilling, spontaneous salute to the guard's courage and indestructibility.

Lombardi did not keep Kramer in the game beyond one quarter—there was no point in overdoing a good thing. But while he was in there he demonstrated that the offensive right guard's slot was his beyond doubt. By midseason he was playing a full game, doing it with gusto and relentless drive. Teamed up with Fuzzy Thurston, his old sidekick at left guard, he and Fuzzy were once again football's "Fearsome Twosome." Kramer's superb blocking was a key element in Green Bay's triumphal march to the NFL title in 1965. And again in 1966 and 1967. And to two postseason Super Bowl victories along the way.

In January of 1968, Jerry Kramer—everybody's All-Pro—was selected by the Philadelphia Sports Writers Association for its Most Courageous Athlete of the Year award. Of the year? Of a lot of years!

7 The Diamond Trump

Pete Gray

IT MIGHT NEVER have happened had the grocer in Nanticoke not bought an automobile. In 1923 cars were still objects of curiosity in that little Pennsylvania coal-mining town and everyone wanted a ride in the new "machine." The grocer didn't mind if the neighborhood kids crowded into the back of the open tourer when he made his daily round of deliveries. Five-year-old Pete Wyshner was the youngest among the joyriders that afternoon. As the automobile approached his corner, Pete realized it was past time for him to go home. Untutored in such matters as centrifugal force or relative speed or the effect of gravity, he jumped from the moving vehicle. Instantly he was hurled to the pavement. His body bounced, whipping his right arm against the vehicle where it became snared in the spokes of the rear wheel.

When Pete regained consciousness in the hospital, cocooned in bandages, his first reaction was fear of his father's anger for the mischief he had got into. Strangely, though, his father was subdued and unusually soft-spoken. Before the boy could sort it out in his fogged mind he lapsed back into sleep. It was two days before he discovered that his badly mangled arm had been amputated. All that remained were a few inches of stump attached to his shoulder.

When Pete was well enough to go home he began to realize fully what it meant to be one-armed. Routine, everyday actions—washing, eating, scratching an itch on his right side, playing with a toy—became major challenges. As he convalesced from his ordeal, Pete found that each day could not be simply lived—it had to be conquered. So, young as he was, he tried to master each day as it came, grappling obstinately for ways to make one hand do the work of two.

By the time fall arrived the aching had disappeared from the stump and Pete had made his adjustments, had found ways to compensate for his loss. His empty sleeve was a nine-day wonder among his schoolmates but that passed when they found he could do almost everything they could—although perhaps not in quite the same way. With each passing month he became increasingly adept and in a year or so Pete was seldom consciously aware that his right arm was missing. He had developed such dexterity and strength in his left arm that he could hold his own among his contemporaries.

This was a time when baseball was still undisputed king of American sports and every boy dreamed of becoming another Babe Ruth. Pete was not immune to the lure of the diamond but he was ignored in his attempts to join in the pick-up games dominating the free time of Nanticoke's younger set. Nobody could really blame the players for not wanting their side saddled with a one-armed baseball enthusiast. Pete hung around the field anyway, watching every play intently, seeking to figure out ways he could imitate the moves despite his missing arm. When there were gaps in the action, he swung a bat on the sidelines trying to make the wood whistle through the air as he whipped it around to meet an imaginary ball. Then the day arrived when every available boy except Pete had been picked and one side was still short a player. In desperation, the team captain told Pete he could play in the outfield. "Just remember," he said, "if another kid shows up you're out of the game."

For the first two innings there was nothing for Pete to do. In the third, a soft grounder came squibbling toward him. Running to meet it, he flicked his glove aside, scooped up the slow roller, and threw to second in time to hold the batter to a single. The next two batters popped out in the infield and the third man struck out. Then Pete's team was at bat and it was his turn at the plate.

Pete grasped the bat firmly, cocking it over his right shoulder as though he had a two-handed grip on it. The first pitch was wild. The next was in the strike zone and he swung with all his strength. He met the ball squarely, driving it over the third baseman's head. While the ball was being fielded, Pete raced for first, rounded it, and made it to second safely. The next man up advanced him to third, and then he scored on a long fly. As he walked away from the plate Pete could feel his heart pounding, not from exertion but from the joy of scoring a run.

Midway through the next inning the game ended when one of the mothers turned up and called her protesting

son away to do some chores. The bat and ball belonged to
him and he took them with him. No matter, Pete was
happy—he had finally broken the ice.

In the weeks that followed Pete was able to play occasionally, although he was always the last one chosen. If
it had not been for his batting he would not have been
picked at all. He had a good eye for a pitch, seldom striking out. His fielding was another story. He couldn't seem
to hang on to a hard-hit ball. He had little trouble gloving
the ball but it would not stay gloved. It would smack into
his mitt and then, without a second hand to close in behind it and trap it securely, it would bounce right out.
Pete, frustrated, would scramble to retrieve the ball and
by the time he had scooped it up and whipped it in the
batter had gone for extra bases.

Angered by his poor fielding, Pete gritted his teeth
with determination every time the ball was batted his way,
snatching hard at it, trying to will it to stay in his glove.
The harder he tried, the more the ball bounced out.
Then it dawned on him that he was making the fundamental error of approaching fielding the way a two-
handed player does. What he needed was to think the
whole thing through in one-handed terms. He mulled the
problem over, substituting reason for wrath. He visual-
ized every move that had to be made and then considered
every possible way a one-armed player might accomplish
it. He acted it out, testing each possibility to see if it
would stand up. Slowly, he fashioned a fielding technique
tailor-made for his physical condition.

To start with, he snipped some of the stitching along
one of the seams in his glove. Reaching in, he removed a
good-sized portion of the padding and flattened down

the rest to reduce the "bounce." Then he tried wearing the glove with his hand thrust only part way in, far enough so that he had control over the "pocket" in the mitt, yet not so far that he could not pull his hand free fast. Next, he practiced flipping his hand up into his right armpit and clamping down on it with his few inches of stump, so that he could snatch his hand away leaving the glove pincered under the stump. When he had that routine down fairly smoothly, he introduced a ball into the act. To begin his move, he tossed the ball straight up in the air. Instantly, he reached for his armpit and clamped the glove off under the stub. Slashing his ungloved hand out, he caught the ball as it was dropping from the toss. Now he was set to throw to the infield.

It would be heartwarming, but inaccurate, to say that Pete was an immediate success when he tried his new technique in actual games. Sometimes the ball bobbed out of his glove before he could go into his juggling act. Sometimes he couldn't unglove his hand fast enough to catch the ball after he had tossed it in the air. But the new technique went right more often than it went wrong. Now he wasn't always the last one picked to play. By the time the snows came to end baseball for that year, he had developed a measure of deftness that was resulting in fairly reliable fielding.

Through the winter Pete continued working on the problem. Still not satisfied with his glove, he went whole-hog, removing all the padding. Now a hard-hit ball would sting like the devil but there was no longer any "bounce" in the glove. For hours on end, he practiced snatching the glove off under his stump, trying to speed it up. When weather and homework permitted, he went into the yard to swing a bat against imaginary balls.

When spring and baseball returned to Nanticoke, Pete was ready for them. He had developed confidence and asked no favors of his teammates or opponents. As far as he was concerned, he could meet them on the diamond on a basis of equality and nobody doubted it after an incident in one game. Pete had hit safely and succeeding batters had moved him around to third. The next man up stroked a sharp grounder toward second. Gambling that he could beat the second baseman's throw to home, Pete raced for the plate. The catcher crouched over the plate, set to receive the throw from second. Ten feet out, Pete dived in headlong, sliding home safely and knocking over the catcher in the process. Both boys scrambled to their feet. Raising his hand menacingly, the catcher yelled angrily, "If you weren't a cripple I'd paste you right in the kisser."

Pete let go with a round-house swing that upended the catcher again. Looking down at the sprawling figure, Pete demanded of him, "If I'm the cripple, how come I'm standing and you're on the ground?"

Pete's devotion to baseball was no passing fancy. With each succeeding season it became an increasingly important part of his life. He was a fixture on the diamond, first to arrive, last to leave. At home he concentrated on exercises he had devised to sharpen his ball-playing reflexes and to toughen his palm for the punishment it received in his unpadded glove. At the very least, when he could do nothing more active about it, he *thought* baseball.

As he moved through his middle teens, Pete clung to every nickel or dime that came his way. There was purpose to his parsimony; when he had saved the price of admission he would hitchhike to Philadelphia, and even to New York, to see a major-league game. For him the highlight of 1932 was hitching all the way to Chicago to see the Yankees win the World Series. Except when there was pressing action elsewhere on the field he kept his eyes riveted on his idol, Babe Ruth, imprinting on his mind every nuance of the great man's techniques.

By the time he reached his late teens, Pete was not simply a good player; he was a very good one. He had become expert in place-hitting, slamming the ball between outfielders for extra-base hits. He was a fast, sure-footed runner—no mean accomplishment for a youth with only one arm because the absence of the limb tends to throw a runner off balance, cutting down on speed and nimbleness. His fielding had become a joy to watch, a thing of beauty, so fast and smooth it was almost a blur. He had long since stopped tossing the ball in the air after gloving it. Now when he snared the ball in his unpadded glove he rolled it up on his chest, clamped his mitt free under his stump, swept his bare hand back across his chest to pick off the ball, and fired it to the infield—all in one continuous, fluid motion. He had a strong, accurate throw and was able regularly to nail players who tried to beat out his throw from the outfield. Pete also had something else going for him—style. He played with verve and daring, making "impossible" leaping, stabbing catches. But then, he was conditioned to the "impossible" because baseball itself was supposed to be beyond the realm of possibility for anyone lacking an arm.

It is hard to say when Pete first began to harbor hopes of breaking into the professional ranks. He knew that cracking the majors was a one-in-a-million shot, even if he possessed a whole body. Yet, he had his dream and it would not go away. It moved a small, tentative step closer to realization when he began to play with area semipro teams. It was a far cry from the majors but at least it was a notch above the sandlots. He moved into a little better caliber of baseball in 1940 when he began playing with the Bay Parkways, a Brooklyn semipro team of considerable merit. It was around this time that he switched his name to Gray. He had no fault to find with Wyshner but Pete Gray seemed to have a more "basebally" ring.

As lead-off man for the Parkways, Pete Gray batted a thoroughly impressive .449 in 1940. This sort of thing doesn't remain quiet for very long, especially when it is coupled with good field play. Word got around that the one-armed outfielder for the Parkways was worth watching, not just to see something unique in the way of ballplayers but also to see some first-rate ball. Professional scouts came to Brooklyn to see for themselves if the stories were true. They were, and the scouts liked what they saw. But they hesitated. After all, who had ever heard of a one-armed professional ball player?

In 1942 Pete Gray got his chance to try to make the grade as a pro. He was signed by Three Rivers of the Canadian-American League, not the big time but nevertheless a professional league, if only barely so. And Three Rivers was managed by Mickey O'Neill, which was important. There was little that O'Neil did not know about the sport and he had the knack of passing his lore along to his players. If they had the basic talent, he had the faculty for showing them how to make the most of it.

O'Neil worked with Gray patiently, skillfully, trying to

polish his play to a professional sheen. Pete had been very good; now he became even better, both in the field and at the plate. Under O'Neil's tutelage he developed new adroitness in "dragging" a bunt, imparting backspin to the ball at the moment the bat makes contact so that the ball "drags"—stops rolling forward prematurely— making it harder to field and giving the batter an extra split second to make it to first safely. Pete batted .381 that season, leading the Canadian-American League. O'Neil predicted that even better things were in store for his left fielder. The fans, once they recovered from the initial shock of seeing a one-armed player, looked at his performance instead of his body and they agreed with the manager.

Pete had his toe in the door of the majors and he managed to push it open a little wider in 1943 when he moved up to the Memphis Chicks of the Southern Association. Some of the Southern Association players were youngsters on their way up, some were veterans who had had their day in the majors but still had some sound baseball left in them, and some were just good journeymen who had reached the highest level to which their talents could carry them. But all of them—the ones climbing the peak, those past the peak, and those halted on a plateau—had hustle and savvy and a competitive spirit. Pete was now moving in fast company. This was the time and the place that would make or break him, and he knew it.

Determined to make good, Pete gave it everything he had. He played smart ball, aggressive ball. In the field he moved fast, making leaping, spearing catches that were thrillers to watch. The only balls that ever got by him were sizzling line-drives rifled to his right, or "unarmed"

side, and there were few of them because he had an un-
canny way of wrenching his body around to backhand
them with his left. His throws were accurate and strong,
his hitting sharp. Once he was on base safely, he was
always a threat to steal. He looked good on the diamond;
there was no doubt of that. Then, when everything
seemed to be going his way, he got himself put out of
commission by a vicious slide home. He beat out the
throw to make the score but he came away with an assort-
ment of lacerations and bruises, especially to the only
hand he possessed. So, in the middle of his hot streak, he
had to be benched to give his damaged hand a chance to
heal.

After Pete returned to the lineup it took a little while
for him to work back into his stride again. The season
ended on an inconclusive note for him—he had shown
that he was good but he had not yet convinced the majors
that he was good enough for them.

Pete came on strong in his next season with Memphis,
and he stayed strong in game after game. In one bitterly
contested duel with the Chattanooga Lookouts, neither
team had been able to get onto the scoreboard by the late
innings. Pete Gray came to bat. He looked the first pitch
over carefully. It was low and outside and he let it go by.
The next pitch was also low and he let that one go by too.
The third one was right in the groove. He met it hard
and squarely with his big, 38-ounce bat, clouting the ball
in a tremendous arc that cleared the 20-foot fence 330
feet from the plate. His homer won the game for Memphis.

That was the kind of ball Pete played all through that
season. He ended 1944 with a solid .333 batting average

and led the league in stolen bases with 68. The Southern Association voted him its Most Valuable Player. Even if he never played in another game, he had achieved a moment of glory as a baseball pro. But there was more to come. The door finally opened all the way for him—the St. Louis Browns signed him to their roster. He had done what only a minute fraction of all the two-handed aspirants ever succeed in doing—he had made it to the top of the baseball ladder; he had made it all the way from a mangling accident on the streets of Nanticoke to major league baseball.

Even if Pete Gray should live to be a hundred, he gathered enough thrills and excitement during the wonderful season of 1945 to last him through all his declining years. Wherever he went he was the darling of the fans, even those pulling for the opposing team. Luke Sewell, manager of the Browns, would shake his head over Pete's spectacular catches and mutter, "I still don't believe it." Pete picked up the nickname of "The One-Armed Wonder," and everybody sang his praises. Mostly because of his ability to jerk the fans out of their seats with his sensational plays, he was the talk of baseball. Partly, though, his name was on people's lips because he had become more than a ballplayer, he had become a symbol and the country was in need of a symbol like him.

The United States was now in its fourth year of World War II and one sad result was the growing numbers of veterans with empty sleeves or flapping trouser legs. Pete Gray was an antidote to the despair that accompanied the mutilations of the battlefield. He demonstrated that the loss of a limb need not be the end of the world, and he did it with a blaze of magnificence. Like the time the

Browns were deadlocked in a tie game with the Philadelphia Athletics in that unforgettable 1945 season.

The Browns had one man on, there were two out, and the batting order had worked around to Pete. The lanky six-footer stepped into the box and took his stance with his bat cocked on the right on a level with his head. The pitcher took his windup and rifled a fast ball. Timing it perfectly, Pete swung hard and met it squarely. A roar burst from the stands as the ball ripped into the outfield for a double, driving in the winning run for the Browns. That is the sort of memorable moments the lad from Nanticoke gave baseball.

There was never to be another season like 1945 for Pete Gray. He had reached the zenith of his sports career and now the shadows were starting to lengthen. When they put together their 1946 team, the St. Louis Browns were bound to make room on their roster for established players returning from the just-ended war, and something had to give. St. Louis traded Pete Gray to Toledo of the American Association. While Toledo was making its contract offer to Pete, the Mexican League tried to lure him away to play ball south of the border. Neither offer appealed to Pete. He and baseball had given each other a golden moment and that was the way he wanted it to be remembered. He wanted to go out as a big leaguer. Pete Gray decided to go home to Nanticoke.

Pete Gray had class.

8   The Rivals

Tenley Albright and Carol Heiss

Never before, or since, had the world of figure skating seen such a thrilling contest for supremacy on the ice. Superb on their flashing skates, Tenley Albright and Carol Heiss electrified spectators as each strived to surpass the other. What made this brilliant rivalry truly gripping for the audiences was the knowledge that they were witnessing a drama that contradicted logic, a drama that only a few years earlier would have been impossible to contemplate. It was made more absorbing by the series of curious twists that had intertwined the extraordinary careers of the two ice queens.

The very beginning of the drama was in the winter of 1944 when each—Tenley in Newton Center, Massachusetts; Carol, 200 miles south in Ozone Park, Long Island—donned her first pair of skates. Tenley was nine; Carol was only four. Both, displaying a natural sense of balance, were at once at ease on the blades, instinctively confident. They had expected ice skating to be fun and they were not disappointed; they found all of the amusement and thrills they had anticipated. They also found something more—an inner urge to master the ice, to dominate it, not merely to play on it. Thus, simultaneously in New York and in Massachusetts, the stage was being set for the two girls to start out on what would become a collision course.

Impressed by Tenley's agility and by her enthusiastic though futile attempts to execute figures, her father bought her a proper pair of figure skates and took her to the Skating Club of Boston for lessons. It was at the Club, an internationally recognized center of skating know-how, that she grasped for the first time the intimidating demands that the sport imposes on those who seek seriously to attain proficiency in it.

To the layman, figure skating seems like ballet on ice and the skaters like a dance troupe on blades instead of ballet slippers. That is only a half-truth. Figure skating *is* theater, but first it is precise science, mathematically exact and rigidly inflexible. The foundation of the sport is an awesome 68 school figures, each a meticulously plotted, subtle variation of the figure 8. To skate competitively, every entrant must be capable of executing each of the 68 school figures because the initial segment of all competition requires performance of six figures chosen by random lot. The next segment brings out the theatrics, the eye-arresting, gravity-defying loops, spins, and leaps performed—dancelike—to music of the skater's choice. At that time school figures counted for 60 percent in scoring, free skating only 40 percent.

Glimpsing what figure skating is really about is often enough to discourage most beginners from any serious attempt to conquer the ice. Tenley was different, undaunted by gruelling practice sessions that stretched ahead endlessly, undismayed by perfectionist, hard-to-please instructors. When she fell, which was often, she simply climbed back to her feet and tried again. When others took breaks, she continued working, fascinated by the intricacies of the figures and determined to learn to execute them with the disciplined precision the coaches sought. Gradually her falls became less frequent, her flaws in execution less apparent. Club coaches began to single her out for special attention, recognizing that she had the will—and perhaps even the talent—to become a good figure skater.

Meanwhile, out on Long Island, Carol had been gripped by the same fervor for figure skating. Her mother took her to the Junior Figure Skating Club in New York to see if she could be accepted for lessons. The coaches—Pierre and Andrée Brunet, a husband and wife team who had been Olympic champions before turning to teaching—were surprised and pleased by Carol's zeal as she skated for them, attempting by instinct alone to duplicate the maneuvers of the older, experienced skaters twirling around her. They agreed to take her on as a pupil.

Each girl was a joy to teach—avidly absorbing instructions, grateful for criticism, enthusiastically practicing hour after hour and day after day. The effort was showing results; they were gaining a measure of proficiency in the loops, brackets, and counters that are peculiar to each of the compulsory school figures. But much more is required than mere mastery of the mechanics of the figures; at heart it is a question of quality of performance. In a race the first one across the finish line wins and in football one touchdown is as good as another, but figure skating is judged from an entirely different perspective. Successful execution is only a starting point; after that it is up to the judges to evaluate the merit of the execution on the basis of the precision and finesse with which it has been performed. The competitor must not only skate a required pattern but must strive to trace it in the ice with perfect fidelity to its prescribed configuration. Moreover, it must be traced with the proper edge of the blade because inside and outside edges leave slightly different signatures and these are scrutinized minutely in evaluating quality of performance. Tenley and Carol listened attentively as their coaches explained these fine points and each worked out on the ice obsessively, seeking to achieve the level of skill and grace called for. Then disaster struck Tenley.

For two days she had been feeling listless and tired. When her temperature shot up to 102° and hovered there, her father—puzzled by the symptoms and concerned by them—called in a specialist. His diagnosis was a shock—polio!

Tenley was rushed to the hospital. After intensive testing, the outlook became a little less ominous. The polio was confirmed but this was a relatively mild case. Still, polio in any form leaves its mark on the victim. In Tenley the disease caused cellular damage in her back, seriously weakening the muscles in that part of her body.

Before the month was out, Tenley was permitted to go home, after it was agreed she would return to the hospital every second day for physical therapy to counteract the inroads of the disease. Between treatments she was to perform at-home exercises to supplement the therapy. Uncomplainingly, Tenley followed the routine that had been laid out for her. She was especially diligent in following the prescribed home exercises because she was resolved that the disease must not come between her and her skates. Only two months after she had been stricken she had recovered sufficient strength to resume her lessons. She was a bit shaky the first time out but that soon disappeared. That was in November.

The Eastern Figure Skating Championships were scheduled for Philadelphia in January. Partly as a reward for her persistence and partly because they believed her performance would be creditable enough to provide encouragement, her instructors suggested that Tenley enter the junior division of the Eastern. Excited and awed at the prospect, she agreed. Her performance was more than merely creditable—it was the best in her class. Remarkably, only four months after the polio attack she became the Eastern junior champion.

Two hundred miles to the south, Carol was also making solid progress in the quest to become an accomplished skater. Week by week, her performance was becoming noticeably better and the New York coaches could perceive in her the same promise, the same unwavering determination, that the Boston coaches could see in Tenley. The striking parallel between the two became inescapable in 1949 when Carol, like Tenley before her, was stricken by disease. In Carol's case it was an especially virulent attack of whooping cough that ravaged her.

So devastating was her illness that for a time the doctors despaired of saving Carol's life. Finally the crisis passed and she began to respond to their ministrations but recovery was an agonizingly slow process. It was a year before she could lace on her blades for the first time since the onslaught of the disease; she could not hide her anxiety to learn what it had done to her skating.

Surprisingly, the long layoff had not affected her performance. True enough, there were some cobwebs but once they were brushed away she showed no loss of agility or of form. Certainly she had lost none of her zeal for the sport. Her instructors, more than ever convinced that she had a bright future on the ice, intensified the training schedule to make up for lost time.

In 1950, Carol notched her first important, competitive victory, winning the Middle Atlantic junior title. Jubilant over her showing, her coaches entered her in the more demanding Eastern championships. Performing with a maturity remarkable in one so young, she won the Eastern junior championship. Soon after Carol gained her Eastern crown, Tenley won the national junior championship. But Carol, too, now entered the national picture by winning the U.S. novice championship.

The sports press began to sit up and take notice of them, praising the performance of each. Inevitably, a number of observers compared their quite different styles and speculated on what would happen when the time arrived that they skated against each other. It was the kind of speculation that ice buffs thrive on because the two slender blondes, alike in so many ways, were studies in skating contrast. Tenley was the classicist, the purist, poised on her blades with her shoulders arched back, her movements fluid and controlled. Carol was the dynamo, fiery and fast, leaping as though jet-propelled, her ponytail whipping in circles as she whirled with abandon.

A significant turning point in their careers came for each of them in 1952. Both skated extremely well at the Nationals at Colorado Springs. Tenley left Colorado with the U.S. senior women's title, Carol with the U.S. junior women's crown. On the strength of these victories each was selected for the American team at the World Championships at Davos, Switzerland, in February, 1953. Though each skater would be a member of a national team, each would be skating in individual competition for the World title. Thus, for the first time, Tenley and Carol would be in head-to-head competition.

The field at the World Championships is always intimidating because all are international-class performers, but for the U.S. skaters there would be the additional psychological burden of knowing that no American girl had ever won the World title. When the meet got under way the weather added another dimension of testing for all the skaters. The temperature flirted with the bottom of the thermometer and a bitter wind gusted down from the mountains to buffet the performers.

The meet was divided into a two-day segment for the compulsory school figures, followed by a final day for free skating. At the end of the initial segment Tenley held the lead in school figures, Carol trailing several places behind her. On the third day each contestant was alloted four minutes for her free-skating routine. Carol skated first, putting on a dazzling display that brought spectators to their feet. Good as she was, when Tenley's turn came she was even better. The seven judges awarded her a unanimous victory; Tenley had brought America her first World women's title. Carol was awarded fourth place in the strong field, adding to the jubilation of the U.S. team.

Within weeks the two rivals met again when they contended for the North American crown in Cleveland. Again Tenley was the victor but this time Carol, closing in on her, emerged in the runner-up spot. Before the year was out they skated against each other once more, in the

Nationals where Tenley was defending her U.S. title. Nothing changed—Tenley was the winner, Carol the runner-up. Then in early January, 1954, when both were tuning up for the World meet in Norway, tragedy struck Carol for the second time in her young life.

It was a freak accident during a practice session, a collision with a skater when both—backs turned to one another—decided at the same moment to attempt a whirling turn. In the collision Carol's left leg was slashed deeply by the other's blade. At first the injury did not appear to be too serious, but when Carol returned to the ice after several days of rest her leg buckled under her. A thorough examination revealed that a leg tendon had been severed. It seemed unlikely that Carol would ever again be a competition skater.

Carol refused to accept the discouraging medical opinion because to be denied her skates was unthinkable to her. Citing Tenley's exercise therapy to overcome polio, Carol insisted that the same kind of effort would do for her what it had done for her long-time rival. Doctors conceded that it *might* reverse the damage but they were not optimistic. Carol, on the other hand, had no doubts. She began a rigid schedule of bending, flexing, and stretching the injured leg, massaging the calf, and taking daily walks—each one a little longer than the one before—then she progressed to jogging. At first the leg pained acutely from the constant, hard workout it was receiving, then the pain subsided. Slowly, and then at an accelerating rate, strength and agility returned.

While Carol was busy repairing the damage to her leg, Tenley was having her own troubles at the World meet in Norway.

It was the last day of competition and Tenley had built up a commanding lead in defense of the crown she had won in Davos the previous year. Approaching the climax of her free-skating routine, she was just coming out of a stunningly executed combination axel and double-loop jump when she slipped and sprawled on the ice, shocking the arena. That fall cost her the title. In Davos, when she had brought America its first World women's title, Tenley had been exultant; now, having had the prize escape her grasp so ignominiously when it had been all but cinched, she was disconsolate.

Fans on both sides of the Atlantic now hashed and rehashed intriguing questions. Had Tenley Albright reached her peak and commenced an irreversible descent from the heights? Had Carol Heiss' severed tendon ended her career on the ice? Was the gripping rivalry at an end?

All questions were answered three months later in Los Angeles, scene of the 1954 Nationals where Tenley would be defending her U.S. women's title. Confounding the pessimists who had counted her out, Carol entered the meet to challenge Tenley for her crown. Both girls skated brilliantly. In the school figures—always her strong point—Tenley was poised and controlled, executing the figures with hairbreadth precision, her movements flowing into one another with classic grace and beauty. In the free-skating segment—Carol's strong point—the challenger performed her dazzling spins and rocketing leaps with the thrilling abandon and speed that had become her trademark. The outcome was the same as it had been in the Nationals of the previous year—Tenley retained the title, Carol came in second. The fans had gotten their money's worth and they knew now that they had not seen the last of the rivalry.

The highlight of 1955 was the World Championships, this time to be held in Vienna. Both Tenley and Carol were keyed up and tense as it commenced. For Tenley, after losing her crown in her fall in Norway, there was the strain of knowing that no woman had ever been able to regain the title once she had lost it. For Carol there was the knowledge that no matter how well she performed she had yet to beat her rival. But when they glided out on the ice, each forgot everything except the present and the immediate challenge.

Tenley's performance was inspired, so close to perfection that it left spectators breathless. Carol was able only to gain sixth in the school figures but in the free skating she was magnificent, soaring in defiance of gravity, looping and whirling with blurring speed. Her remarkable exhibition lofted her into second place in the final standings but again it was Tenley who was first, reclaiming the World crown that had slipped from her grasp a year earlier.

As 1956 dawned, the attention of the sports world focused on Cortina d'Ampezzo, the resort town perched in the Italian Dolemites where the Olympic Winter Games were to take place. The two perennial rivals had, of course, been selected for the U.S. team. Carol, who turned sixteen at Cortina, was the youngest girl ever to skate for the U.S. in Olympic competition.

Just before the Games commenced Tenley had an accident reminiscent of the one that had severed Carol's tendon. The surface of the practice rink at Cortina had become pitted; her skate struck one of the rough spots, jolting and swinging her left foot up so sharply that the blade cut deep into her right calf. Team doctors dressed the wound carefully, hoping for the best. Though the injury was painful, Tenley could not afford to rest because to do so would run the twin risks of going stale and of having the leg stiffen up. So she continued to practice for the few days remaining before competition began. By opening day the wound had started to heal and the pain had gone.

Twenty-one skaters were entered, all of them trained to a fine edge. As she had done so consistently in the past, Tenley dominated the school figures. But Carol, exhibiting more finesse and precision than ever before, was a surprisingly close second. The fans, realizing that Carol was a powerhouse in the free skating, excitedly anticipated the next phase of competition.

Tenley skated first. Her four-minute performance, exquisitely executed, was spectacular. When Carol glided out an hour later she, too, treated the fans to four minutes of pure spectacle; one reporter termed it "the most daring program ever skated by a woman at the Olympics." The judges, with hard decisions to make, deliberated long before announcing their scoring. They gave Tenley a razor-thin margin of victory in the free skating, 169.6 to Carol's 168.1. She had brought America its first-ever gold medal in the Olympic event, and Carol brought home the silver.

The long, hard competition between the two and the closeness of their Olympic finish, fired up the fans for their next meeting only two weeks later in the World Championships at Garmisch-Partenkirchen, West Germany. The press stirred the fire hotter by reporting that the rivalry had become a bitter feud, something both girls denied firmly. Other contestants at Garmisch, good as they were, received scant attention—all eyes were fixed on the two blondes from the U.S.

Both girls skated magnificently. At the conclusion of the school figures Carol, for the first time ever, held a narrow lead over Tenley. On the last afternoon of the meet the atmosphere at rinkside was electric with excitement. As the free skating commenced, the two principals in this drama on ice reached for all the gems in their repertoires and displayed them in all their brilliance—split jumps and delayed axels and solchows, double loops and double flips, spins, spirals, leaps. Heedless of the snow that had commenced falling, the fans watched in awe, well aware that it was unlikely that any rink would ever again present two such masters. The ovation for each of them was so thunderous and sustained it was difficult to hear the loudspeakers announcing the judges' scores. Then the word penetrated through the stands—Carol Heiss had edged out Tenley Albright. Finally, after so many years of rivalry, their roles had reversed and Carol was the new World champion.

The two would meet again in a few weeks in the Nationals in Philadelphia and this time Tenley would defeat Carol and then retire from competition. Carol would go on to win the World and U.S. crowns for three consecutive years and would claim the gold medal in the 1960 Olympics. But those who witnessed the stunning duel between Tenley Albright and Carol Heiss at the rink in Garmisch in 1956 maintain that that was the year women's figure skating had two World Champions simultaneously.

9   Rolling Back

Alonzo Wilkins

Even as an infant, Alonzo Wilkins seemed destined to become an athlete. Visitors to his family's modest home in Washington, North Carolina, claimed that they had never before seen a baby squirm, wriggle, and crawl as powerfully and rapidly as that chocolate-brown bundle of nonstop energy.

The boy scarcely slowed down when he started school in that pleasant, little city on the Pamlico River. The only time he actually sat quietly was when he was at his desk poring over his schoolbooks. Otherwise, his life was one of jubilant, irrepressible movement. Gradually, all of his classmates came to take it for granted that he would be the one to set the pace for them in games they played during recess. After school when the youngsters chose up sides for a playground basketball game everyone wanted to be on Alonzo's team—it was good insurance against being stuck with the losers. When the boys went down to the banks of the Pamlico with cane poles and a can of worms, it was almost always Alonzo who pulled in the most and the biggest fish. And when they shinnied up trees just to work off the exuberance of youth, it was Alonzo who generally went highest and fastest.

By the time Alonzo entered high school he had developed into a lithe, well-muscled youth with quick coordination and stamina. Those were all qualities, together with his quick mind, that brought smiles of happy anticipation to the coaches. Under their tutelage he assimilated the finer points of basketball, football, and track, and became an outstanding performer on all three teams. He was that rare athlete who could achieve the delicate balance between concentration and relaxation, bearing down without tensing up. The key to his smooth, fluid performance on hardwood, gridiron, or cinder track was simply that he enjoyed what he was doing. Not that he was not serious about meshing his talents and his supple body to sink baskets or snake-hip his way downfield or cross the tape first; he just didn't make the mistake of taking himself too seriously.

In 1950 Alonzo Wilkins graduated from high school, one of the finest all-round athletes the school had seen in a long time. Nobody was a bit surprised when he was offered a full sports scholarship by Winston-Salem State Teachers College.

It was difficult to resist the temptation of a scholarship that would mean a college education plus a chance for athletic competition on the collegiate level, but there was something else Alonzo felt he had to do first. In the same week that he graduated from high school, the bitter Korean War broke out and America was gearing up for the conflict into which it had been plunged. For Alonzo, his course of action seemed clear: he enlisted in the U.S. Army.

The same coordination and stamina that had turned him into a standout athlete made Alonzo Wilkins the kind of recruit that drill sergeants always hope to find. After he completed basic and advanced training, he emerged as a polished, reliable soldier. Toward the end of 1951 he received his overseas orders. After one short, last leave at home he was ready to cross the Pacific on his way to war.

Midwinter is not the time to pick for an ocean crossing, not if one is looking for gentle ocean swells and balmy breezes. Almost from the moment the troop transport left the Golden Gate Bridge astern, it ran into dirty weather that hung on day after day. On the ninth day out, halfway across the Pacific, the ship was struck by a wild storm that caused it to shudder, roll, and dip drunkenly. Sick bay was crowded.

Several hours after the storm struck, Alonzo was going down a ladder from one deck to another. He was careful to hold both handrails as he descended. He was in midstep when the vessel gave a violent lurch, breaking his hold on the rails. He tumbled to the deck, slamming his back hard against the sharp edge of one of the steel ladder treads.

For a brief moment, the wind knocked out of him, he felt nothing. Then pain locked him in its vise. It was several minutes before he was able to climb awkwardly to his feet in the deserted companionway. Half doubled over, he managed to shuffle from support to support until he reached his bunk. He toppled into it and tried to will the pain away. He could have called for a medic but he kept his misery to himself, waiting for the pain to subside.

But the pain did not go away; it simply changed character slowly from a sharp knife piercing his middle to a dull ache making every little movement a giant obstacle. By the time the ship docked in Japan it had eased a bit, or perhaps it only seemed that way because Alonzo was getting used to its presence.

Assigned to a troop unit in northern Japan, he was glad to be away from the transport and back to dry-land soldiering. He plunged into his duties and tried to forget the nagging pain that seldom disappeared from his body.

The heavy snows in northern Japan were an annoyance to Alonzo's unit, making the going slow and difficult. But for him the problem was especially acute because the treacherous footing aggravated his aching. Ironically, the snows had diminished and there was even a hint of spring in the air when he slipped on an ice-slick path and fell heavily. As he struck the ground the hurt in his back erupted like smoldering ash whipped into flame. Gasping, Alonzo tried to struggle to his feet. He could not move!

Lying there, face pressed into the snow, he tried to force his arms and legs to close in under his body and lever him erect. He could move his arms but his legs remained outstretched at a crazy angle, refusing to obey his commands. Tears of frustration welled in his eyes, the cords in his neck stood out from the effort he exerted so futilely. Almost five minutes passed before he was discovered and carried to the dispensary.

Hampered by their limited facilities, the base doctors evacuated Alonzo to a better equipped hospital in Tokyo. There it became apparent to the medical authorities this was a case that required the attention of Stateside specialists, so they flew him to Walter Reed Army Hospital in Washington, D.C.

A battery of Walter Reed experts examined Alonzo carefully, then they rechecked their findings to rule out any possibility of error. Their verdict was devastating: three discs in the spinal column had been crushed during the fall aboard ship months earlier. The doctors could imagine the intense pain that Alonzo must have suffered in all that time and they marvelled at his fortitude in bearing it so secretively. It was difficult for them to tell him that an operation could offer only a slim chance of success. They would utilize every shred of skill they possessed, they told him, but the damage was so severe they could hold out little hope. "Operate," Alonzo said firmly.

The operation failed. Alonzo knew that instinctively as soon as he regained consciousness. His listless legs, seemingly no longer a part of him, told him that. The doctor in charge of the case, hating every word he had to utter, confirmed what his patient had already guessed. Alonzo posed only one question, "Can't you operate again?"

There was compassion on the doctor's face and in his voice. "Yes, we can try again, but the chance of success will be no greater than before and probably will be poorer. I must tell you that the odds are great that you will be left a paraplegic, unable to control your limbs or organs from the waist down."

Alonzo did not hesitate. "Operate," he said.

The surgeons could not have tried harder. Alonzo realized that and he did not hold it against them when the second operation failed also, leaving him a paraplegic.

Lying in bed recovering from the rigors of his two operations, Alonzo had a lot of time for thinking. He did not waste it in grieving for himself. "What was done was done and all the self-pity in the world couldn't alter that," he says. "If the doctors couldn't fix me up, it was a sure thing that tears wouldn't do it."

Coming to grips with the situation, Alonzo faced reality squarely. His body was crippled and it would stay that way until the day he died. But that did not mean he had to make things worse for himself by developing a crippled mentality to go along with it. He was only nineteen; most of his years lay ahead and it was up to him to make the most of them. As he lay in bed gathering strength, he made a pledge to himself that he would learn to adjust to life with half a body and would make the functioning half perform double-duty to compensate for the portion he could no longer use. He has never broken that pledge.

In 1953 he was transferred to the Kingsbridge Veterans Hospital in The Bronx, New York, for rehabilitation. He had already learned how to use a wheelchair competently but now, under the guidance of experienced therapists, he began to find out how to make it a virtual extension of himself. He learned the knack of swivelling it around smartly, negotiating tight places, rolling up and down ramps. He acquired deftness in levering himself in and out of the chair unaided, and in doing from a sitting position all of the ordinary, everyday things that people usually do standing or kneeling or bending. He never complained nor indulged in feeling sorry for himself; he was much too busy trying to restore himself as much as possible to a normal life.

For him, a normal life included athletics and he did not intend to let his useless legs deny him the joys and thrill of participation in sports. Kingsbridge Veterans Hospital has a well-equipped gym designed to serve the needs of "sit-down" athletes. The most popular gym activity is its wheelchair basketball program. It was natural for Alonzo to gravitate to the hardwood court. Learning the rules of "wheelie" basketball was not difficult; developing the ability to play the game well with a rolling chair substituting for running legs took considerably longer. But he had been too good an athlete for too long not to make the transition. Slowly, he adjusted to the confinement of his wheelchair, retraining his reflexes to accommodate to his vastly altered condition. He hadn't lost the eye-hand coordination or the passing and shooting accuracy that had made him a schoolboy basketball star. Now, once again he sparkled on the hardwood, sinking baskets from under the net or from outside, whipping bulletlike passes, racing downcourt and then pivoting on a dime to elude the opposition.

Enlarging his athletic repertoire, Alonzo also began working out regularly on the hospital track, training himself to spin his wheels fast and straight. Wheelchair racing is not simply a matter of bearing down on the wheels harder to make them whirl faster than the other fellow's; it is also a matter of how the spin is imparted to the wheels. Each hand must bear down simultaneously with matched pressure or else the chair veers off course, losing precious time. It is quite a knack and Alonzo mastered it. Practicing as diligently as he had when his flashing spikes carried him pounding along a cinder track, he developed the speed, stamina, and coordination to become a great wheelie racer.

But Alonzo Wilkins had a goal that embraced much more than athletic accomplishments—he meant to become a self-supporting, responsible citizen who could make his own way in the world independently. He wanted to escape reliance on a dole to satisfy his material needs and to do that he knew that he must have a marketable skill. Assessing all of the possibilities, he narrowed his choice down to watch repairing as the likeliest prospect. He had discovered enough about the watchmaker's art to realize that it is an exacting, precise occupation requiring dexterity, patience, accuracy, and close coordination of eye and hand—qualities that he possessed. He also knew he would have something else going for him—his determination to succeed.

In early 1956, Alonzo Wilkins enrolled in the Joseph Bulova School of Watchmaking in Woodside, New York. He had not come expecting to find a magic formula for instantaneous success and so he was not dismayed by the long, arduous course. Step by step he began to learn all the techniques—reading blueprints and complex diagrams, using precision tools, making miniature solder joints, operating a jeweler's lathe, working on balance wheels, hairsprings, escapements. He studied theory, watch design, jewelry fabrication, engraving. He tackled watches put awry by the resourceful instructors, and he made them tick again. When he graduated from the school in 1958 he was an accomplished watchmaker, ready to meet the world on its own terms. Renting an apartment in New York City, he set aside one room as a repair shop. It was not very long before word-of-mouth advertising about the excellence of his work brought him enough customers to assure a comfortable living. He was standing on his own two feet, so to speak, and it felt good.

Even while he was undergoing his rigorous training course Alonzo had not forsaken athletics. With the independence provided by operation of his own business, it became relatively simple to arrange a work schedule that allowed time for sports on a regular basis. Now, however,

his devotion to athletics took on a new and deeper significance. He felt an obligation to encourage other paraplegics to utilize sports as he had—as a path leading back
into the world. To achieve this end, he began making
rounds of hospitals in the New York area—driving his
own hand-controlled car—to put on demonstrations of
his prowess in the gym. His enthusiasm, self-confidence,
and dexterity acted on his audiences like a tonic. He
could succeed with paraplegics where able-bodied therapists had failed because he was one of them and he had
made good. He was the indisputable proof that wasted
limbs need not mean wasted lives.

"Take it from me," he says with deep conviction, "a
wheelchair can be a trap if you let it. It can restore mobility to the body but it can immobilize the spirit. Confined
to a chair in a world of the able-bodied, a person finds it
terribly easy to feel self-conscious and conspicuous, even
freakish, and to retreat from the world. This is where
sports become so important. Once a paraplegic can be
persuaded to participate, he gets caught up in the excitement of the game and forgets all about spectators. Af-
terwards he remembers that those spectators cheered him
on—not as some sort of oddity but as a competitor who
can win if he tries hard enough and has the skill. Once
that registers with him, he is on his way back into the
world."

When Alonzo wheeled through the wards, a friendly
smile lighting his face and encouraging words on his lips,
or when he gave one of his masterful wheelie demonstrations, he radiated an atmosphere of confidence and
promise that enveloped all those around him. And when
he left to go to another hospital, some of that atmosphere
remained behind to buoy up the patients he had been

trying so adroitly to entice to the therapy of athletics. Watching Alonzo at work one afternoon, one of the doctors observed astutely, "He and his gym work out to be a part of the curriculum at every medical school. It adds an entirely new dimension to therapy."

Alonzo Wilkins, a man who followed his own advice, entered as many wheelchair athletic meets as he could fit into his crowded schedule. In the National Wheelchair Games of 1957, 1958, and 1959, in Bulova Park, New York, he walked away—wheeled away, if you insist on strict accuracy—with first place in both the basketball free-throw and the 60-yard dash.

The watchmaker-athlete-therapist even became a sports figure of note abroad by turning in winning performances in the International Paralympics, the quadrennial Olympics for paraplegics. In the International Paralympics in Rome in 1960, and again in Tokyo in 1964, his sterling performances in various basketball and track and field events drew cheers and won him a chestful of gold and silver medals. Alonzo saw no reason why he couldn't remain active and successful in athletic competition for many years to come. As he observed with wry humor, "After all, I'll never be slowed down by fallen arches or varicose veins. Name me one able-bodied athlete who can make such a confident prediction."

If you were to return to the banks of the Pamlico to hunt up some of his childhood friends, they would tell you that they always knew that even with half a functioning body Alonzo Wilkins would still be a fine athlete. You would have to add that—with legs or without—Alonzo Wilkins is a whole man.

10 Bantam Ben

Ben Hogan

Some GOLFERS ARE BORN with the winning touch, with that natural affinity for the game that creates instant harmony between them and golf. Bobby Jones had it. Walter Hagen had it. Gene Sarazen had it.

Ben Hogan didn't have it. The slender, five-foot-eight Texan—who could shoulder his golf bag and still not top 150 pounds—was no born golfer. His movements on the course didn't flow with natural, effortless grace. He didn't have the physique for booming out tremendous drives. He couldn't relax on the links, couldn't force the tension from his diminutive body. All in all, he should have been a Sunday golfer, happy if he was able to break 90. Yet, Ben Hogan not only became a champion, but a great one. The greatest, many say, and it is hard to dispute them.

When Ben was born in 1912, the last thing the Hogans would have had on their minds was golf. Coping with the practical problems of keeping food on the table and a roof over their heads was what they thought about. Even if they had been able to pursue the sporting life, in their circles in the country out from Fort Worth, Texas, golf

141

was a foreign taste, like anchovies or impressionistic paintings.

When he was nine, Ben's father died and his mother brought him and his older sister and brother to Fort Worth to a rundown but affordable neighborhood on the east side of town. City living was no magic path to solvency; food on the table and a roof overhead were no lesser problems in town than in the country. To ease the burden, Ben hustled a newspaper route. He was nudged into golf when he discovered he could make more money caddying than delivering papers.

Ben was a good caddy. He was patient, willing, and anxious to please. Quietly and tirelessly, he walked the course with his burden of clubs, never intruding on the golfers who had hired him yet always at their elbows when they wanted him. The more serious players began to seek him out as they discovered that the pint-sized caddy would never disturb them with distracting chatter.

If Ben was serving the players well, they were at the same time serving him well. Without realizing it, they were serving as his coaches. Ben watched them closely—their stance, their grip, their swing, the clubs they selected for a particular shot. He looked for the reason why one could drive farther than another, or loft out of a trap so much better. Before he was able to save enough to buy himself a set of clubs, the young caddy had played the course countless times in his mind, swinging an imaginary club in unison with the golfers he watched, mentally imitating their strong points and avoiding their weak ones.

Ben Hogan was in his early teens when he was able to obtain his first set of used clubs. Though he was left-handed, those pick-up clubs were right-handed. Since he couldn't change the clubs, he changed himself, forcing himself to adopt a right-handed stance.

Now that he had clubs of his own, he set out to play on the ground all of the rounds that he had played in his mind. Other caddies would relax between calls for their services, but not Ben—he played golf when he wasn't shouldering someone else's bag. The trouble was, he didn't play well. For one thing, he had to accustom himself to thinking and reacting right-handedly, which is easier said than done. He had his work cut out for him in trying to overcome the clumsiness that went with his switch from left to right. For another thing, he discovered that—awkwardness aside—what worked for many of the golfers he tried to emulate did not work for him. He could mimic their drives faithfully yet his ball would carry only a fraction of the distance of theirs. Ultimately he realized that they drove the ball with a 180-pound or 190-pound physique behind their swings, but his lightweight build was no match for theirs. So he began experimenting in a search for ways to compensate for the weight disadvantage he would always have.

It would be a mistake to get the idea that the novice golfer was all liability and no asset. His first major plus was his determination, his will to succeed. It was this that kept him on the course when fatigue clamped itself around his legs and arms and across his shoulders. His second great asset was an unusual capacity for concentration. He could exclude all extraneous thoughts from his consciousness, filter out all distracting sights and sounds. Focusing on the specific problem he was wrestling with at the moment, he created a wall around himself so that nothing else intruded.

Weeks lengthened into months and became one year, then two and three and still Hogan's dedicated search for excellence was unflagging. His game had become smooth, competent, good enough to earn the respect of local golfers. But he was not content to be merely good, so his ceaseless practice continued.

The young golfer was a fixture on the course, like the fairways and the sand traps. His palms grew hard and horny from the unremitting practice, his fingers developed calluses that split and pulled away from the flesh painfully, but he did not let up on the workouts. This single-minded willingness to push himself mercilessly moved his game up several notches. More and more, he carried home trophies from the amateur tournaments he entered. Trophies are fine and Hogan did not scoff at them, but he had his sights set higher—his aim was to be accepted into the ranks of the Professional Golf Association and to try for the rich rewards for those who can climb to the top of the PGA circuit. He took the leap into professionalism in 1934.

It took courage as well as ability to play the PGA circuit. It is a wearying grind with no quarter asked or given. It is a couple of days here, playing your heart out against the toughest competition the game can produce, and then a quick trip to another tournament for more of the same. For six, frustrating years Ben Hogan worked his way around the professional circuit without a win. Six hard, out-of-the-money years in which he took the crushing disappointments and the constant pressure and came back for more. After each day's play the others went back to the clubhouse, but he stayed out on the course to practice all of the shots that had gone wrong for him. Over and over again, he worked with his putter, his irons, his woods, seeking perfection. At night, he soaked his hands in a brine solution to toughen them for the beating he was giving them.

Other players took occasional vacations to put golf out of their minds for a while and to let tension and fatigue melt away. Not Hogan. He couldn't afford the luxury of idleness because he now had a wife to support. A pillar of strength for her husband during this long, dismal period of failure, Valerie never complained or lost faith in him. Her constant encouragement, and his own stubborn refusal to accept defeat, kept him going. Sometimes, though, money was so scarce that he had to pawn his clubs to bring home groceries. Whenever things sank that low, he took odd jobs to build up a small stake to keep them going. Then he got his clubs out of hock and went back to the PGA tournaments and to the grind of his interminable practice.

In his seventh year on the PGA tour Hogan's persistence bore its first fruit—he started to play up among the winners. Once he had broken the ice, he came in among the leaders with reasonable regularity. It was reward for his lean, frustrating years of sacrifice and strain. At that point he could have eased up just a little but Hogan was not ready to relax his punishing pace. He was driven by something within him to fight to the very top, not to be among the best but to be *the* best. So he continued to practice hour after hour in his pursuit of excellence.

At all the stops on the PGA tour Hogan was now a center of interest. Sports writers were coining names for him: "Bantam Ben," "The Hawk," "Texas Ben." Now when he teed off, the little, intense golfer wearing the linen cap that had become his trademark had his full share of the gallery. The spectators were respectfully silent while he examined the lie of the ball, studied the terrain ahead, decided his strategy, selected his club, addressed the ball, swung. As the gallery applauded, Hogan was already thinking of his next shot, turning the problem over in his orderly, analytical mind. He was not unappreciative of the applause. It was simply that for him there were only two protagonists—the course and himself—and all else was unimportant.

Success is fickle—today's winner becomes tomorrow's loser. In early 1946, Bantam Ben's game began to falter. A disastrous hook crept into his drives. The ball took off low and hard, then it came down fast and hooked to the left. He tried all the standard remedies—opening his stance, experimenting with his grip, cutting the ball at the moment of impact, using more left-arm motion in his swing. They reduced his hook but they also cut as much as 10 yards from his drive. One flaw is as fatal as another; there was no advantage in trading a hook for a shorter drive. Hogan dropped out of the circuit and returned to Fort Worth to wrestle with his deteriorating game.

For four days he did not touch a club, a long layoff for him, and simply studied his problem from every possible angle. On the fourth night, lying awake in bed, he had a brainstorm: pronation. Years earlier Scottish golfers, seeking to correct hooking, had touted pronation—a hand movement that opens the face of the club on the backswing and closes it on the downswing so that it has returned to its original position as club meets ball. Modern players had long ago abandoned pronation as old-fashioned and unsound. But was it? Lying in bed dredging up the discarded technique from the past, Hogan conjured up two refinements: adjusting his grip very slightly to the left, and cocking his wrist a trifle on the backswing to open the club face to its widest.

He was on the course early the next morning to put pronation to the test. It worked beautifully. The ball took off in a high, straight, long arc and then settled down lightly with no trace of a hook. He practiced the technique for a solid week and his driving was spectacular. Rejoining the tour in time for the rich Tam O'Shanter, Hogan led the field and followed up this win by taking the Western Open.

From then on, Bantam Ben was virtually unbeatable, moving from success to success and crowning his streak by taking the coveted United States Open in 1948. He was now the acknowledged national champion, hailed by experts as the finest golfer in the world. More than twenty years had elapsed since the skinny, awkward, left-handed caddy had dreamed his first dreams of conquering the sport. He had finally attained his goal and all of his struggles seemed to be behind him. They were not.

On a foggy morning in February, 1949, Ben and Valerie were driving back to Fort Worth from Phoenix. They had passed the crossroads town of Van Horn in west Texas and were climbing a long rise on U.S. 80, headlights on to pierce the soupy fog. As the car topped the rise, two pairs of headlights abreast bore down on it from the opposite direction. A Greyhound was attempting to pass a truck and both vehicles spanned the entire road—collision was unavoidable. In the split second before the head-on crash, Hogan twisted himself in front of Valerie protectively. His instinctive action to shield his wife miraculously saved her from serious injury. It also probably saved him from instant death because the steering wheel slammed deep into the backrest where a moment earlier he had been sitting. But Bantam Ben was only barely alive—bones shattered, flesh torn and mangled. The doctors performing the emergency procedures on that mutilated body were pessimistic.

Hogan clung to life tenaciously, fighting to recover. Then a fresh blow struck—blood clots formed in his system. Specialists performed a delicate operation to tie off a number of vessels—including the *vena cava,* the great artery running through the trunk of the body—hoping to bottle up the clots in the tied-off sections. This placed additional strain on the golfer's punished body because now other veins and arteries would have to do double-duty to compensate for the by-passed vessels. Bantam Ben faced this additional challenge in the only way he knew—with fortitude and refusal to accept defeat. After a touch-and-go period, he began slowly to mend.

Messages of encouragement flooded in, even from people who didn't know a 9-iron from a curling iron, because it doesn't take sports savvy to recognize courage. Golfers among the well-wishers were reconciled to the sad fact that the great pro would never again play competitively but they were grateful merely to have him among the living. One of Hogan's gloomiest moments came when he returned to the United States Golf Association the trophy he had won in the 1948 U.S. Open with the regretful message that he could not defend his championship that year.

By summer he was back on his feet, shaky and weak but at least no longer flat on his back. Concentrating on working the shakes out of his steps and on learning not to favor the ankle that had been broken, he commenced leg exercises and massages. Each night Valerie gave him a rubdown and bandaged his legs. Gradually, the muscles began to feel alive again and the stiffness faded from his joints.

In the fall, Bantam Ben went out on the course and began practicing short chips and putts, playing rolls from different positions. Having a club in his hands again had a tonic effect on him. He progressed to working from the practice tee, starting off with short irons and then moving up to the woods.

Eleven months after the accident, Hogan turned up at the Los Angeles Open. Everyone was delighted to see him back, even though he would be relegated to the ranks of the spectators. But Hogan hadn't come to watch; he confounded everyone by entering the tournament. He didn't win—an eleven-month layoff is too great a handicap even for one who has not been a wink away from death. Even so, he played a solid, eminently respectable game. Bantam Ben was not yet a has-been.

The doctors cautioned him against extending himself so soon but, familiar with the character of their patient, they did not really expect him to heed them. They were right—Hogan pushed himself as relentlessly as ever, continuing on the pro tour and practicing hard between tournaments. His goal was the 1950 U.S. Open, a pressure-cooker kind of contest that few believed he would enter. The odds-makers calculated that even if he had the temerity to enter he could not be rated a serious contender for the national championship he had been unable to defend one year earlier. What they neglected to realize was that the Merion Golf Club in Ardmore, Pennsylvania, where the Open was to be played, is trickier than most courses and for that very reason was attractive to Hogan. Merion places a much greater premium on strategy, control, and judgment than on sheer power and daring. It is Hogan's kind of course, suited to his scientific, reasoned kind of game.

From the moment he stepped up to the first tee at Merion, Bantam Ben was oblivious to the spectators and, indeed, even to the other contestants. His universe had shrunk to the terrain from tee to cup and he allowed no one and nothing to intrude upon it. He was the Hogan of old, calculating each shot with scientific precision, assessing every factor—the slope of the land, the angle of approach, the effect of the breeze, the "grain" of the grass. If the physical strain took its toll of his damaged body as the day wore on—as it must have—he did not allow it to reflect in his play. He was masterful, but he was playing in a field of masters. At the conclusion of regular play, the tournament was deadlocked in a three-way tie among Lloyd Mangrum, George Fazio, and Ben Hogan. The championship would be determined on the following day in an 18-hole play-off of the three leaders.

The next morning the course was thronged with spectators who appreciated the high drama of the moment. Everyone wondered whether Bantam Ben, after the taxing 36 holes of the previous day—his first 36-hole day since his accident—could continue his pace. Would he falter as play wore on? Would his control weaken, his judgment waver, his accuracy become flawed? Hogan must have been aware of the questions the 10,000 spectators were asking themselves.

All three players seemed evenly matched on the outgoing 9 holes. At the turn, Hogan and Mangrum were tied at 36 with Fazio only one stroke behind. By the time they reached the 15th hole, Bantam Ben led Mangrum by one and Fazio by three. At the 17th, his hold on the lead had increased to four strokes.

An excited gallery lined the long, par-4 18th. Fazio went one over for a 5. Mangrum made it in 4. Hogan made it in 4. Ben Hogan, the man for whom golf was thought to have ended between the headlights of a Greyhound bus, had done the incredible—he had regained the national championship with a remarkable 69.

There were other great victories for Bantam Ben—his record includes four U.S. Opens in all, a British Open, two Masters, and two PGA championships—but after his dramatic feat at Merion in mid-June of 1950 all else has to be anticlimax.

11　The Good Life

Paul Berlenbach

N<small>EW YORK CITY</small> at the turn of the twentieth century had a split personality—it was the Big City but it was also a collection of small-town neighborhoods, many of them built around immigrant groups preserving their Old World customs. One of these groups took root in Astoria in the Borough of Queens; you could recognize it by the German accents, the German food shops, and the *Turnverein*. A very Germanic institution, the *Turnverein* was a social and civic center. Most of all, though, it was a gymnasium—not a gym in the American sense of team sports but rather a place for developing the body by working out on the gymnastic equipment.

The Germans have always been very big on physical culture and the *Turnverein* was seldom free of minor shock waves generated by the body-builders flinging themselves about enthusiastically. But among those gymnasts there was one who stood out from the throng because he seemed to sweat and strain more than the rest, never stopping for a breather when the others did, never moving on to the next piece of equipment until fully satisfied with his performance on the last piece. For young Paul Berlenbach it was not merely gymnastics—it was communication. Through his body, he was trying to say to the others, "See? Here, at least is something I can do well." It was the only way he could speak to them. He was a deaf-mute.

Until he was two, Paul had been like any other normal child, then he was stricken with a severe case of scarlet fever and for two days his life hung by a slender thread. After the crisis passed and the illness began to recede, it left behind a terrible reminder of its visit. Paul could no longer speak or hear. It was one of those things you can't account for, the doctor said, and there's nothing to do but learn to live with it.

Grieving because Paul had been condemned to a prison whose bars were a tongue that could not speak and ears that could not hear, his parents sought ways to penetrate it. They invented hand signs for big and little, hot and cold, thirsty, hungry, good, bad, and similar basics, and they repeated the signs endlessly until finally the boy realized what they represented. It was not a great deal, but at least it did permit rudimentary communication on essential matters. It was quite another story outside the house. In the midst of chattering children, Paul alone was silent, unable to understand or to be understood. The young are impatient and unthinking in the face of the abnormal, and Paul was abnormal. His silence and his lack of reaction when spoken to meant only one thing on the streets of Astoria. The children began calling him "Dummy" and said he ought to be locked up with the rest of the crazy people. Paul could not hear the epithets but the meanings were all too clear to him.

After he started to school his situation did not improve. The teachers had neither the time nor special training to enable them to teach a deaf-mute, so he sat imprisoned in his silent world, learning only the odd fragments that his eyes alone could grasp. The only special attention he received was from classmates trying to think up bigger and better ways to ridicule him. That is why the *Turnverein* became so important to him, why he worked so purposefully and endlessly to master the gym equipment. It was the only way he could prove to the world, and to himself, that there was some merit in him.

Paul gradually filled out and grew tall. His shoulders broadened and he became hard-muscled. An atmosphere of authority, of sureness, came over his gymnastic performance. His movements were methodical, even slow, but speed is not the essence of gymnastics—strength is, and Paul had developed strength. Little by little, the epithets and gibes died away. Paul was achieving the goal he had set for himself; he was demonstrating that there was indeed something at which he could excel.

One summer afternoon when Paul was fifteen he was working out at the *Turnverein* as usual when a short, violent storm ripped through Astoria, sending numerous tree limbs crashing to the streets. Returning home after the storm, Paul found a limb blocking his path. He began climbing over the obstacle, unaware of a downed power line caught in its branches. His body brushed the wire. There was a puff, a crackle, and he was felled by the electricity jolting through him. Passersby, using poles, levered the unconscious youth away from the wire.

When Paul came to, he was aware first of the circle of faces peering down at him. And then, stunned by the discovery, he realized he was hearing their voices! He stared at the moving lips, listening spellbound to the amazing music of the words they were forming. Then he drew a lungful of air and yelled. He heard his own voice bellowing out! Startled, the onlookers dropped back. Paul leaped to his feet and ran home, yelling all the way.

At last Paul Berlenbach was free of his prison of silence. But if he could hear and make sounds, he could not yet make speech. The thirteen-year void could not be erased in a single stroke—the sounds he articulated were the dimly remembered babyisms of a two-year-old. His parents joyfully began to teach him how to speak, how to form words, inflect his voice, pronounce tongue twisters. Everything was a lilting, thrilling adventure for Paul now—conversation with others, the ticking of a clock, the clip-clop of the iceman's horse, every squeak and rattle and snatch of sound and, most of all, his own voice.

It was a new Paul Berlenbach who worked out at the *Turnverein* each day, no longer isolated from the others by an impenetrable barrier. He had long wanted to try wrestling but for that you have to have a partner, and in the past he had always been odd man out. Once his speech and hearing were restored, he found that the others would make room for him on the mat. He knew nothing of the techniques of wrestling but he had great strength, patience, and persistence, and they stood him in good stead—it was not very long before he was able to hold his own against his opponents. This was a new, soul-stirring experience for him, this ability to be the equal of those who for so long had looked on him as an inferior, and it infused him with zeal for the sport. Now he lavished on wrestling the same dogged drive for mastery that earlier he had devoted to gymnastics. That persistence, and his powerful body, tipped the scales in his favor. Within a year he was the acknowledged *Turnverein* wrestling champion. The matter would probably have ended there if Nat Pendleton had not intervened.

Pendleton was a prominent amateur wrestler who performed under the colors of the swanky New York Athletic Club. In Astoria one day with time on his hands, he wandered into the *Turnverein* while Paul was wrestling. Pendleton was impressed by the strength of the young giant, liked the way he worked on his opponent with composure, concentration, and persistent application of pressure; he shrugged off all the technical flaws in Paul's performance as things that could be corrected by a good coach. When the match was over, he engaged the sweating youth in conversation, drawing Paul out in spite of his reticence to discuss himself. As they spoke, Pendleton could picture the youth wrestling under the banner of the NYAC.

Few things made members of the New York Athletic Club more jubilant than to see their club colors carried to victory in athletic competition. The trouble was that most of the regular members were well-heeled, well-padded executives whose physical exertions seldom extended beyond working up a little gentlemanly perspiration in one of the exercise rooms. To compensate for this shortcoming, the NYAC granted free memberships to selected amateurs who had the capacity to bring home victories for the club. So the admissions committee was attentive when Pendleton described to them the potential of the young wrestler he had discovered in Astoria. They promptly voted Paul Berlenbach a membership; that vote would completely alter his life.

Paul was apprehensive about going to the NYAC—the club was a world that was strange to him—but Pendleton was persuasive. The decisive factor was his pledge to teach Paul all the finer points of wrestling that could not be learned in the *Turnverein*. He was as good as his word and the pace of instruction he maintained allowed no time for feeling strange in the new, posh surroundings.

Despite his pupil's rock-hard, well-muscled physique, Pendleton started him off on a rugged program of conditioning—weight lifting, calisthenics, lap after lap on the indoor track, and especially head bridges. Head bridges, fundamental to wrestling, enable a downed wrestler to avoid having his shoulders pinned to the mat even though his opponent is straddling him and applying pressure. In bridging, the wrestler pulls his feet and head in under his body and arches his back up from the mat so that all his weight plus his opponent's is supported by his toes and the crown of his head. Over and over, Pendleton grappled with Paul on the mat while the youth bridged them both until the cords in his neck and his legs stood out in bold relief.

Between workouts, Pendleton explained the theory and tactics of the sport, drawing simplified diagrams to make his points clear. Then he squared off with Paul to practice what he had described. For the first time, Paul was learning what top-notch wrestling is all about—the variety and subtleties of take-downs from a standing position, the attacking holds on the mat, the defensive maneuvers from underneath. Pendleton showed him how to apply leverage skillfully, how to execute escapes, whip-overs, scissors, Nelsons, locks, whizzers, lifts, trips. He skipped nothing but he wisely capitalized on his pupil's strong arms and shoulders by concentrating on perfecting arm locks, body lifts, leg lifts, and combinations of those holds. Paul was a good student—earnest, persistent, and strong as an ox. He was not a rapid learner but once Pendleton got his point across, Paul never forgot it. When Paul began to wrestle competitively for the NYAC he brought in victories, just as Pendleton had predicted to the admissions committee. At the end of his first year as a club wrestler he had become the pride of the team. And he was getting better all the time.

In 1920, Paul Berlenbach was selected to wrestle on the United States team in the Olympics in Antwerp, Belgium. When his name was announced, Paul was incredulous. "There must be a mistake," he said to Pendleton. "They can't mean me." But there had been no mistake and the young man from Astoria, bursting with pride, started out on his great adventure. All the way across the Atlantic aboard the S.S. *Princess Matoika,* still half-afraid he might discover it was all a dream, he found odd corners of the deck where he could work out.

When the 1,500 athletes paraded behind their national flags in the new Antwerp stadium, Paul had a lump in this throat to think that he was a part of that grand spectacle. Actual competition began on the following day. Paul wrestled well and in his first few matches he was unbeatable. Then the nineteen-year-old came up against a more experienced, superbly skilled opponent who eliminated him in a hard-fought match. There had been nothing shoddy about Paul Berlenbach's performance and there was no shame in his loss. He had come a long way from Astoria.

Returning home, Paul found a job as a taxi driver and managed to be assigned to the hack stand in front of the NYAC, so that when business was slow he could duck in for a quick session on the mat. In 1922, all the striving paid off handsomely: he won the 175-pound amateur championship of the United States. The regulars at the Astoria *Turnverein* threw out their chests and boasted about their pal, the Champ, erasing from their minds all memory of the misery they had brought him for so many years.

Success did not alter Paul Berlenbach. He still was gentle-natured, unassuming, tooling his taxi through New York traffic and spending all his spare time working out at the NYAC. It was soon after he won the wrestling crown that he began to take an interest in boxing. He walked in to the club's boxing room several times and stood just inside the doorway watching Dan Hickey, the coach, giving pointers to his charges. He wondered about boxing, wondered what it would be like to compete in the ring instead of on the mat. One day he approached Hickey and asked if he would explain some of the basics. The ring-wise instructor looked at Paul curiously for a moment. "It's not for you, kid," he said. "No wrestler has ever made a good boxer, although many have tried. The two things are just too different. Take my advice and stick to what you can do."

"I'm not planning on becoming a boxer, Mr. Hickey. I'm just wondering what it's like," Paul explained. "Won't you please show me?"

Hickey hesitated, then handed Paul a pair of gloves.

Both men laced up and climbed into the ring. Hickey commenced to feint and weave around the younger man, hitting his target at will with stinging lefts and rights. (He later confessed wryly that he had thought it would be a grand opportunity to teach wrestlers that boxers were their betters.) Paul absorbed all the blows with no sign of distress or even discomfort. He simply kept bearing in and striking out at an opponent who eluded him easily. The one-sided fight went on for a few minutes until Hickey neglected to dance away fast enough and a single blow caught him in the midriff. He dropped to the canvas. When he could finally talk, his statement was succinct. "If you can hit like that maybe you are the one wrestler who can make the switch. Lessons begin tomorrow."

That is how it started. Hickey quickly discovered that his new pupil's left was dynamite; his right was good but it wasn't the lethal weapon of his left. Paul was a natural southpaw, which meant that whenever he set himself to lash out with his outstretched, exposed left, he was telegraphing his intention ahead to his opponent. The first order of business was to reverse his stance so that he led with his right and kept his left concealed, cocked and ready to explode. The transition was difficult but Paul kept working on it and gradually became used to a right-handed approach and left-handed follow-through.

Shrewdly deciding that his pupil—lacking the quick moves, the agility, and the dash—would never be a fancy, bob-and-weave boxer, Hickey concentrated on his endurance, his ability to take a pounding, and that beautiful left. He thought that, with proper seasoning, they could be enough. Paul was a joy for the coach to work with—

never complaining or suggesting a break from the rugged routine, never questioning instructions, always putting out his utmost.

When Hickey thought Paul was ready, he matched him against a middling fair amateur. Paul won by a knockout. The following week Hickey sent him against a better light heavyweight. Paul repeated his knockout victory. The instructor felt the first stirrings of excitement. He arranged matches against increasingly better, craftier fighters, and Paul beat them all. By mid-1923 he had fought and won 16 times, 13 of them by knockouts.

Paul was surprised when Hickey suggested that he turn pro. "I'm convinced you can make it, and if you're ever going to try it has to be now," Hickey said. "You are twenty-two and soon it will be too late. It's now or never."

Paul turned pro with Hickey as his manager. Before 1923 was over he fought three times, winning each match by a first-round knockout. In the first ten weeks of 1924, he added seven more KOs to his unbroken string of victories. Then he met Jack Delaney, a lithe, quick, rugged fighter with a strong right-hand punch. There was a good turnout for the bout in the old Madison Square Garden.

The first round was even. In the second, Paul's left found its target and Delaney went down twice. In the third, it was Delaney's turn. He caught Paul with a vicious left-right combination that decked him—the first time in his brief boxing career that he had been on the canvas. Bouncing up at the count of three, Paul knocked Delaney down seconds before the round ended. The fans had expected to get their money's worth and they were not being shortchanged.

As the fourth round began, Delaney moved in fast and

whipped a crashing right to Paul's head. He went down and then climbed to his feet, shaking his head to try to clear the fog away. Pressing his advantage, Delaney rifled a flurry of stinging head shots and Paul went down again. Heaving himself to his feet, Paul reeled toward Delaney, trying to carry the fight to him. Delaney caught Paul on the chin with a hard right and once more he went down. Groggy but determined to go on, Paul levered himself to his feet but the referee called a halt, awarding Delaney a technical knockout.

Back in his dressing room, speaking through bruised and swollen lips, Paul apologized to Hickey. "I'm sorry. I really tried. I'll do better next time."

Two weeks later Paul went across the river to Newark, New Jersey, climbed into a ring, and laid his opponent away in the first round. The following month he repeated the performance in a Brooklyn ring. By the end of the year he had chalked up eight more knockouts. He went into 1925 with the same winning touch.

That spring, Paul reached a new high by knocking out Battling Siki, former light heavyweight titleholder. By now he had more than compensated for his defeat at the hands of Delaney. Fans began clamoring for a match between the Astoria Assassin, as sportswriters had dubbed him, and Mike McTigue, current light heavyweight champion of the world. The papers were signed and the fight was booked for Yankee Stadium on the night of May 30, 1925.

It was an unseasonably hot, muggy night and 45,000 fans were crowded into the stadium. They were all there, the greats, the near-greats and the nobodies—Babe Ruth and George M. Cohan and Big Jim Farley, stockbrokers and shoe clerks, bookkeepers and bookmakers, and an excited contingent from the *Turnverein.* A roar went up when the two principals entered the ring.

From the start, it was all Berlenbach. His close-cropped head sloped forward on his thick wrestler's shoulders, he kept advancing with his characteristic shambling gait, shaking off his opponent's blows easily, striking out methodically and ceaselessly with his right and his explosive left. By the end of the fifth round, McTigue was bloody and bruised, his face and body crisscrossed with welts. In the sixth it became apparent that the champion realized the only thing that could save him would be a lucky knockout, so he let loose almost recklessly, lashing out and hoping that lightning would strike. By the eighth it had become obvious that McTigue had shot his bolt in vain. Paul, as strong as ever, was still crowding him, still pile-driving his left relentlessly. His arms leaden, McTigue was now intent on only one thing—back-pedaling away from his adversary. The judges awarded Paul Berlenbach the unanimous decision and the crowd yelled its approval. The one-time deaf-mute and one-time wrestling champion was the new light heavyweight boxing champion of the world.

Surrounded by his corner men to fend off the milling, noisy fans, Paul Berlenbach left the ring and started down the aisle. Before ducking into the tunnel leading to his dressing room, he spotted the nearly hysterical contingent from the *Turnverein.* He waved to them and shouted a greeting. Life has been good to me, he thought, listening to the cheering. He yelled once more to the group from the *Turnverein* and then entered the tunnel.

12 The Little Giant

Sammy Lee

Sammy Lee learned early in life that he had two strikes against him. He was only four when he found out about the first one. The place was Los Angeles and the time was 1924.

A half-dozen years earlier Soonkee Lee had arrived from his native Korea to study engineering, trying diligently to stretch his limited resources to pay his tuition and still provide the basic necessities for his wife and two daughters. It was, at best, a tight squeeze but after Sammy was born in 1920 it was clear to the elder Lee that he must forsake his studies to devote full time to caring for his growing family. Reluctantly abandoning his dream of becoming an engineer, he began hawking vegetables on the street.

Long hours and frugal living enabled Soonkee Lee in time to save enough to open a small shop. He took Sammy with him as he walked about Los Angeles searching for a suitable vacant store. He found many, but he also found something else—the unreasoning, blind prejudice against Orientals that was common there a half-century ago. Time after time landlords turned him away rudely with no attempt to conceal the bigotry that motivated them to refuse renting to him. For Soonkee Lee it was not a new story, but it was Sammy's first cruel lesson in what it means to be discriminated against because of one's ancestry. Clinging to his faith in his adopted land despite the rebuffs, Soonkee Lee eventually found his shop and established his business, but the lesson Sammy learned at his father's side would stay with him forever.

It was not the last time Sammy would encounter prejudice but it was his most important exposure to that sickness, because out of it there developed in him a competitive spirit, a determination never to become an easy, vulnerable target for the bigots of the world. He took to heart his father's admonition that the best defense against intolerance was to obtain the education that would lift him out of reach of those mired in their own stupid biases. So he applied himself in school, becoming an excellent student.

It was several years before Sammy recognized the second strike against him. From his earliest days in grammar school his drive to succeed had not been confined to the classroom alone—it had also extended to the playing fields. He did well in all games and sports, but especially in football, his favorite. By the time he reached junior high he had become an outstanding linebacker—quick, smart, and aggressive. But when he moved up to high school and went out for the freshman team he discovered that something odd had happened during the summer since graduation from junior high—all the others had gained inches and pounds while he alone had remained the same size. He stood among the other tryouts like a young sapling half-hidden in a grove of tall trees. At only 5 feet, 1 3/4 inches—a height he was never to exceed—he was simply no match for the others. The coach had no choice but to drop him from the squad, despite his demonstrated ability on the gridiron.

In the past the youngster had experienced rejection on racial grounds; now he also experienced it on physical grounds and the twin burden was crushing. Angered and frustrated, he looked for a place where he could shut his problems out of his mind, even if for only a little while. He found what he sought in the neighborhood public swimming pool and more and more he turned to it as his place of refuge.

It is curious that Sammy should have chosen that pool as his sanctuary because racial prejudice was one of its operating principles. Though it was a public facility, it was open to nonwhites on only certain days of the week. This was an affront that Sammy put up with only because here, he thought, at least his small size would not be a handicap. It was not until later that he would learn that in this he was mistaken.

Ironically, the bias that barred Sammy from the pool on certain days now came to his aid as he tried to teach himself to use the diving board properly. Because everyone at the pool on "nonwhite" days was a victim of identical intolerance, there was a bond of sympathy and understanding linking them. It was this that prompted a black youth, seeing Sammy's awkward attempts on the board, to come over to explain some of the basic techniques. This casual encounter was significant because the other youth was a skilled diver and the meeting flourished into friendship that developed a comfortable coach-pupil pattern. With his instinct for athletics and his willingness to practice diligently, Sammy quickly shed his beginner's awkwardness. After several weeks he was performing respectable forward running somersaults and working up to one-and-a-halfs and other more demanding maneuvers. After several months he was diving fully as well as the older boy who had been his teacher.

Impelled by the urge to prove himself in competition, Sammy tried out for his high school swimming team and earned a place on the squad. Under the watchful guidance of the experienced coaching staff, his performance improved markedly. He learned how to use the power of his muscular legs to propel himself from the board in great, soaring leaps, and to use the quick reflexes in his wiry torso to twist into rapid, crisp rolls and snaps before cutting the water cleanly. By his senior year he had matured into a strong, graceful performer bringing in his share of victories in scholastic competition.

None of these victories had come cheaply because he had found that the "nonwhite" syndrome of the neighborhood pool also extended to swimming meets, though perhaps not as openly and blatantly. He had also discovered that his short, squat physique was as much an obstacle on the competitive circuit as earlier it had been on the gridiron. His troubles stemmed from the fact that he broke with U.S. tradition which held that winning divers had to be tall, lithe, broad-shouldered and narrow-hipped Caucasians with blue eyes and blond hair. Here he was, put together in a diminutive, compact package wrapped in olive-yellow skin. Because his race and build were at odds with what tradition-minded judges envisioned, to gain his victories Sammy had to win by a margin overwhelming enough to make the officials accept the unconventional.

Winning in spite of odds stacked against him, the little Korean-American attracted growing attention in scholastic diving circles around Los Angeles. What is more important, he attracted Jim Ryan's attention. There was general agreement among divers that Ryan was probably the most successful and least likeable professional coach in the business. He was abrasive, crusty, short-tempered, and impatient, but he had a remarkably keen understanding of the subtleties of diving. Relentlessly demanding of the athletes he coached, imposing rigid training routines on them, bitingly critical of their performances, he squeezed from them the very best they were capable of giving—provided they had the fortitude to stay with him long enough to give it. Ryan must have liked what he saw in Sammy Lee (and probably found perverse appeal in a short, squat Korean-American taking on the ethnically "correct" six-footers) because he told him gruffly he would coach him.

Under Ryan's stern eye, faithfully following his pithy, explicit instructions, Sammy practiced interminably over the whole spectrum of dives, from the standards to the "show pieces." It was a body-punishing schedule that left him drained, both physically and mentally, as he strived for the perfection that the older man demanded. But it bore fruit. His performance took on new sparkle, crackled with greater authority and precision, whether on the springboard or the 30-foot tower that is often a major stumbling block for divers. In the instant before hurling themselves out into space from the high tower— equivalent to leaping from a third-story rooftop—many are assailed by an involuntary "choking up" that hampers their performance. For Sammy, it was a different story. Controlled and confident on the tower, totally absorbed in the maneuver he was about to execute, he ignored the yawning drop from platform to water.

The grind of practice was not the only stress he was under. He had entered college and was determined to do well, not alone as a matter of pride but also because he meant to qualify for admission to medical school. To be both "jock" and "brain" simultaneously takes more than just talent for each; it also takes the kind of stamina, concentration, and sacrifice that Sammy displayed. Ryan had no quarrel with devotion to studies, but he was adamant in insisting that diving must come first. This became a continuing source of friction between the two because Sammy was just as unyielding in refusing to skimp one at the expense of the other.

As it turned out, he knew himself and his capacity for coping with both challenges better than Ryan did. He forged ahead steadily both as athlete and as scholar. In 1940, entering the junior division of the Amateur Athletic Union's national diving championships, Sammy won the title and immediately entered the open division, coming in fourth against the older, more experienced contestants. Clearly, the "Yellow Peril"—the nickname he had acquired in aquatic circles—had emerged as a power on the American diving scene.

Going into his senior year at college, Sammy Lee was a tired young man, worn by too many high-pressure days straining for success at the pool and on the campus. Yet, despite weariness of body and mind, he could not slacken his pace because 1942 was a critical year for him on both fronts—he was out to nail down both the AAU senior title and acceptance into medical school.

The AAU championships were held at two different sites that year—the springboard events at New London, Connecticut, and the tower events at Columbus, Ohio, since the New London pool was too shallow for deep dives from the high platform. At New London, Sammy was brilliant on the springboard, blending strength and grace masterfully. He emerged with the springboard crown firmly in his grasp, the first nonwhite to do so. A week later in Columbus he was again superb—daring, confident, and letter-perfect on the high tower. The national tower title fell to him, giving him possession of the two most important U.S. diving championships. The following month he entered medical school at the University of Southern California. All in all, it had been quite a year for the little Korean-American.

There was no question now of continuing in active diving competition; the pursuit of a medical degree is too all-consuming to allow any distractions. But, reluctant to abandon the pool completely, Sammy managed to eke out enough time for an occasional intensive practice session that kept him in reasonably good shape.

During his third year at medical school he took time out from the lecture hall one day to attend a local diving event that had attracted many prominent contestants. After the meet he got into a conversation with the then U.S. diving champion. A tall, blue-eyed blond fitting exactly the idealized vision of the way the classical American diver is supposed to look, the champion stared down at the little Korean-American and told him arrogantly that even on his best day Sammy would not have been able to beat him.

That touch of arrogance was a spur that pricked Sammy deeply, deciding him to try for a comeback. He stepped up his practice sessions to the absolute maximum he could manage without putting his studies in jeopardy. In June he was granted the medical degree he had worked so hard to earn. Simultaneously, he was commissioned a first lieutenant in the Army Medical Corps and was assigned to intern in a Los Angeles hospital.

An intern's life is no bed of roses, but at least the ordeal of medical school is behind him. To that extent, the new Lieutenant Lee was able to lengthen his pool workouts and to bring a greater degree of concentration to them. Gradually, he could feel his timing sharpening, his leaps soaring with greater strength, his snaps and twists becoming more fluid. When the 1946 national rolled around he was ready to make the defending champion eat crow.

Sammy drove down to San Diego, site of that year's championships, and for two days he dived with the same kind of daring, precision, and catlike reflexes that had enabled him to sweep the 1942 nationals. His performance was extraordinary, especially on the tower where the high point of his exhibition was a dazzling 3½ running somersault that he had conceived. There could be no doubt of the judges' verdict—they awarded him the title unanimously. The "Yellow Peril" was back in business, goaded out of retirement by the overbearing champion he had just vanquished.

Having done what he had set out to do, Sammy Lee

was satisfied once more to retire from active competition. He immersed himself in his hospital work because merely to be a doctor was not enough for him; he insisted on becoming a top-notch doctor, so he devoted himself to absorbing everything that the hospital could teach him.

For two years he remained away from swim meets. Then, in 1948, the lure of the Olympics began to tug at him irresistibly. What was especially tantalizing to him was that no American of Oriental ancestry had ever won the Olympic diving title. Deciding to make the attempt, Sammy plunged into an intensive conditioning program to regain his form. Then he entered the American team trials and earned a place on the U.S. squad.

Looking around at the divers he was pitted against at the London Olympics—the finest that each country had been able to produce—Sammy realized he would have to be at his peak to stand a chance of beating them. Waiting his turn, he rehearsed his dives mentally, picturing the varied demands each would impose, reminding himself of the split-second timing critical to this one, the vaulting leap that had to lead into that one. When his name was finally called, he quieted his inner turmoil and got to work.

Sammy Lee turned out to be unbeatable that day. His timing and rhythm were flawless, his dives crisp and soaring, daring but beautifully controlled. The spectators knew, even before the judges made it official, that he had won the gold medal. At 5 feet 1 3/4 inches, he was by far the smallest of the contestants, but on that day he became the giant among the world's divers.

After London, Lieutenant Lee returned to his military duties and put competitive diving behind him. He was quite content to be just a recreational diver and to devote himself entirely to ministering to the sick and injured.

Three years after his triumph in London, three years in which he had not entered diving competition, Sammy—by then it was Major Lee—discovered that diving was still not ready to let him go. The coach of the U.S. swimming team, planning for the 1952 Olympics in Helsinki, put it in succinct terms. Without Sammy, he said, the swimming team's Achilles' heel would be its diving; with him—if he could regain his old form—the team would stand its best chance of topping the strong foreign competition. It was difficult to turn down a plea couched in those terms. It was also difficult to resist the challenge of trying for two successive Olympic crowns, something no diver had ever been able to do in the entire history of the Games. Sammy agreed to make a comeback try.

Nobody knew better than Sammy how iffy the whole thing was. He would be almost thirty-two at the time of the Games, old for an Olympian. He would have to give up completely any semblance of a private life to commence at once a nonstop routine of the most intensive kind of conditioning. And after all that, even if he could regain his old form, he could blow it all and fail to make the squad if he had an off-day at the required qualifying trials in New York.

Keenly aware of the odds against him, Sammy Lee returned to the springboard and high tower with a single-minded drive that even carping Jim Ryan would not have been able to fault. For weeks there was only nagging frustration for him. His body ached constantly from the beating it was taking, and he was edgy from the strain of striving for a level of performance that obstinately eluded him. Then, things began to fall into place. Little by little, sharpness and timing returned. Coil-spring responsiveness began flowing back to reflexes that had gone stale. His short, muscular legs commenced to rocket him into soaring leaps with their old power. The magic was still there.

Unaccountably, some of the sparkle disappeared from his performance at the final team trials. Only three of the divers would be granted places on the U.S. swimming team and at the end of the springboard event he stood fourth in the rankings. Everything was riding on the outcome of the tower dives. If Sammy were outstanding enough he could lift his total score enough to put him on the team.

In midafternoon on the final day of the qualifying trials, Sammy climbed the tower for the high dives that would determine whether he went to the Olympics or went home. He was superb—the Lee of old. His right to a place on the team was settled beyond question.

Poolside observers at the Games in Helsinki took account of Sammy's age, of the several interruptions to his diving career, and of the extremely high caliber of the international competition, and cast him in the role of underdog. But Sammy confounded the so-called experts. Putting on a virtuoso exhibition capped by the thrilling 3½ running somersault, his trademark, he garnered 156.28 points in the final round to 145.21 for Joaquin Capilla, of Mexico, his closest rival. He succeeded in doing what no diver before him had done—he won the Olympic gold medal for the second time.

Once shunned for his Oriental heritage and scoffed at because of his diminutive build, Sammy Lee returned to a hero's welcome. The irony of his tumultuous reception was not lost on him, but he responded with characteristic graciousness, dignity, and modesty. He had always been his own man in adversity; he remained his own man in success.

There was more irony in store for him. The United States had taken up arms to try to stem the Communist invasion sweeping down into South Korea. Soon after his Olympic victory, the Army Medical Corps assigned Major Lee to minister to casualties at the 121st Evacuation Hospital in Korea. (He was so good a doctor that when South Korean President Syngman Rhee was ailing it was Major Sammy Lee to whom he turned.) Prejudice forgotten, the land of his birth had become allied with the land of his ancestry and he, a healer in uniform, was a symbol of that alliance. After the war ended, the State Department—anxious to strengthen U.S. relations in the Far East—asked him to undertake an official tour of Pacific nations as unique, tangible evidence of American ties to the Orient. He accepted the mission, fulfilling it with devotion, quiet pride, and success.

Despite what the tape measure may have read, little Sammy Lee was a giant.

13 Hercules

Jim Hurtubise

It HAPPENED at the fourth turn of the one-mile, asphalt-paved racing oval at Milwaukee's Fairgrounds Park. It came with stunning swiftness on the 52nd lap. None of the 36,285 fans thronging the stands that sunny, June Sunday in 1964 would ever—could ever—forget those few heart-stopping moments. But that is getting ahead of the story. The beginning of it is in North Tonawanda, a small town in upstate New York within fall-out range of wind-driven soot from Buffalo's smokestacks.

It was as a teenager in North Tonawanda that Jim Hurtubise developed his enduring passion for cars. Throughout his high school years, after classes he made a beeline for his father's gas station to help man the pumps and, especially, to peer over the shoulders of the mechanics to learn all he could about their craft. An apt pupil, before long he was fully competent to make repairs on his own. With money saved from his after-school job, he bought an old car, fine-tuning and souping it up until it could hit 100 on a straightaway. Weekends, if the stock cars or the midgets were running at Buffalo, he was at the track early and lingered late, enthralled by the contest of car against car, driver against driver. That was how it started.

The scene shifts next to Florida's Tampa Bay area where Hurtubise was assigned for duty when he enlisted in the Coast Guard following graduation. Again he bought a car that had seen better days and rebuilt it from the ground up, giving it more muscle and quicker responses than it had had when new. Then, whenever he could get liberty from the base, he headed with his rebuilt car for the little dirt tracks around the Florida panhandle and tried his luck at stock car racing. He did pretty well for a raw novice, winning a few races. But, win or lose, he came away from every track a little wiser, a little more adept in coping with the demands and the hazards of racing.

By the time his enlistment expired, Hurtubise had an incurable case of racing fever. He hit the East Coast dirt tracks and county fair ovals, then worked his way cross-country, racing as he went. In California in 1955, now twenty-three and a veteran of hundreds of bush-league races, he switched to open cockpit sprint cars where the competition was keener and more experienced, the cars faster. But Hurtubise, no longer the neophyte, had acquired his share of track wisdom, both behind the wheel and under the hood, and he chipped away at the competition, trying his utmost to make it through to the big time.

It was a hard, wearying grind. There were endless hours working on the car, trying to nurse it to a new peak of performance capability. There were the emotion-draining, body-bruising contests on the track, straining to outmaneuver and outrun the field. There were the crushing setbacks when, with victory almost within grasp, the win is suddenly snatched away by a faulty gasket or a fouling plug or a bolt that gives way. There were the long spells when either the car or the driver got fed because there was not enough money for both. But there were also victories—joyous, marvellously satisfying wins with purses that reduced the accumulating bills. And, at last, the wins began to come with a little more regularity. Hurtubise was making progress. He moved up to races sanctioned by the International Motor Contest Association and then to United States Auto Club meets.

There are major milestones along the glory road winding toward Indianapolis and the Indy 500, the USAC's most prestigious, richest race, the one that every driver on the circuit dreams of someday winning. One of these milestones is Sacramento. In September, 1959, Jim Hurtubise won the Sacramento 100 and the victory earned him a bid to the Indy 500.

As they had every May for the half-century since the classic began, the faithful of the racing world converged on Indianapolis for the 1960 rites of the 500. By its very definition, auto racing is a contest of speed. Yet, within that context drivers develop their individual styles. Some tend toward conservatism, running a race built around strategy and finesse, biding their time as they seek the precisely right moment to pounce on the leaders. Some run a more daring race, not reckless but less deliberate, more all-out. They are what track buffs term "chargers," drivers who floorboard the gas pedal from the start and only ease up on it rarely and reluctantly. The gruelling Indianapolis race is a gripping spectacle because it is a struggle for supremacy among the sport's finest and fastest, its wiliest strategists and its most audacious chargers.

The crowd quickly discovered that Jim Hurtubise was a charger, floorboarding the pedal aggressively. In the qualifying heats he set new one-lap and four-lap records that nudged above 149 miles an hour. The cheering fans dubbed him "Hercules," a nickname that was to stick with him.

Only in a Hollywood script would a racer win the Indy 500 his first time out. This wasn't Hollywood—"Hercules" finished 18th. Still, his strong showing earned him Rookie of the Year honors and the satisfaction of knowing that he had joined the ranks of the track elite, even if only as a junior member. From then on, all the major meets invited him to enter.

That fall Hurtubise charged into the lead at Langhorne and never relinquished it, emerging the victor in the 150-mile race. In the spring he was back for the 1961 Indy 500. For 34 thrilling laps every driver on the track was forced to eat his dust. Then, on the 35th lap, the pistons on his straining engine burned out and "Hercules" had to give up the lead and the race. But three months later he held the lead from first lap to last to bring off the win at Springfield. In 1962 he returned to Indianapolis for the big Memorial Day race and this time he went the distance, ending the Indy in 13th place with an average speed of 135 mph. That fall he repeated his Springfield win of the previous year.

Everyone—pit crews, press, fans—knew that the 1963 Indy would be one for the books. They knew it from the moment that Jim Hurtubise teamed up with the Novi, the supercharged, 800-horsepower V8 that had more muscle, more raw power than any other car ever built. But the big red monster was skittish, unpredictable, and no one yet had been able to harness all its brute force to ride it to victory; some who tried had been killed in the attempt. Now the charger and the supercharged would test each other's mettle.

Going into the first turn at Indy, the Novi was seventh in the field of 33. Coming out into the backstretch, Hurtubise floored the gas pedal. Like a spurred stallion, the monster roared and plunged ahead, streaking into the lead at an astonishing 175 mph to put together the fastest first lap in the history of the 500. The Novi was almost a blur as "Hercules" kept up the scorching pace lap after lap around the 2 1/2-mile oval. Finally, in the 102nd lap an oil leak put an end to the remarkable display. The wild ovation that saluted Hurtubise as he steered the disabled car off the track ripped through the arena like an artillery salvo.

After Indianapolis there was no question about it— "Hercules" was the hottest, most exciting driver on the pro circuit. So when he accepted a bid to the running of the 100-mile Rex Mays Classic in Milwaukee the fans counted on getting their fill of daring, wide-open racing. But they also had another reason to expect a real pressure-cooker on the track—the 22 starters included A. J. Foyt and Roger Ward, both of them brilliant, two-time winners of the Indy 500. Only a few minutes into the race it was clear it would live up to advance billing. It was also clear it would be a three-way battle among Hurtubise, Foyt, and Ward, with all the rest looking up their tailpipes.

Down the straightaways and around the turns, engines blasting out shock waves of thunder, the trio punched its way through the light fume-haze almost as one multi-bodied vehicle. The laps clicked off with none of the three able to gain more than a momentary, infinitesimal lead. The spectators, gripped by the unfolding drama, yelled themselves hoarse.

On the 52nd lap it is Ward, Foyt, and Hurtubise in that order and with less than a yard of daylight separating one from the other. Then somewhere in the straining power plant under Ward's hood, something malfunctions. Instantly, his machine loses speed, sways from side to side. With the lightning reaction of a true professional, Foyt manages to steer clear of Ward. Hurtubise, who had been closing the sliver of space separating him from Foyt, also reacts lightning-fast, trying desperately to swing wide of A. J., who is simultaneously swinging wide of Ward.

Hurtubise almost makes it, almost but not quite. His left front tire touches A. J.'s right rear tire and climbs up over it. Foyt's car is unhurt but his vaults high into the air. It stays airborne for a moment; then, like a giant projectile, it smashes head-on into the concrete barrier around the track's outer perimeter. Metal crumples like paper as the car is compressed in on itself. One of the front wheels, torn loose by the impact, whips back, crashes through the cockpit and strikes Hurtubise. Three of his ribs snap, his right lung collapses, blood sloshes into his chest cavity. A spark ignites the alcohol-mix racing fuel and the driver is trapped in the inferno that his smashed vehicle immediately becomes.

Rescue crews tear toward the flames, reach them, begin spewing jets of smothering white powder from their extinguishers. The track ambulance squeals to a stop, sirens wailing, medics leaping out. The flames, choked off, snuff out. Urgently yet carefully, hands reach into the blistering hot wreckage, flip open Hurtubise's harness buckle, gently extricate the maimed, semiconscious driver.

At the hospital the doctors looked at their incinerated, mutilated patient and shook their heads dolefully. It was the massive burns that worried them most. In the whole country only a handful of highly sophisticated medical centers specializing in burn treatment could give that terribly charred racer any hope of survival. One of the handful was the U.S. Army's Brooke General Hospital at Fort Sam Houston in Texas and, thanks to his Coast Guard service, Hurtubise was eligible for admission. An emergency call to "Fort Sam" started an air evac team winging to Milwaukee to pick up "Hercules." On the flight back to Texas the plane's medics, trying to buy time, inserted a tube into their patient's leg to restore some of the vital body fluids seeping out of every segment of his carbonized flesh.

At Brooke, Hurtubise was wheeled immediately into the sterile, intensive care unit. Springing into action, the doctors transfused him with plasma, whole blood, dextrose, and other solutions, injected him with antibiotics, cleared his chest cavity and reinflated his lung, and dressed his appalling burns with sulfamylon. After that they could only wait and hope and repeat their emergency measures at intervals. It was three days before they were reasonably confident of their patient's survival. Now the burn specialists could begin the complex undertaking to try to reconstruct that incinerated body.

It was a task of discouraging dimensions. More than 42 percent of the body had sustained second- and third-degree burns—the legs from ankles to thighs, much of both arms, the nose and cheeks, and the hands, especially the hands. "Hercules" was taken to surgery for the first of what would become a seemingly endless round of operations. This initial surgery focused on the hands to remove dead tissue that could never be revived. The next operation a few days later was to encase those hands in a temporary protective covering by sewing dog-skin grafts to them. Future permanent grafts would be attempted from undamaged skin areas from his own body.

Midway in his second week at Brooke it was deemed safe to remove Hurtubise from the intensive care unit and to embark in earnest on the reconstructive program that had been formulated for him. Mornings were mainly for the extremely painful but unavoidable high-pressure sprayings to flush away minute fragments of dead tissue from raw body surfaces. In the afternoon came whirlpool bath treatments for the arms. And every eighth to tenth day came another grafting operation. No longer of dog-skin, the grafts were now sections of skin cut from Hurtubise's own back, buttocks, and abdomen, so that gradually even those body areas that had come through the gruesome accident relatively unscathed became a mass of wounds.

The pain was constant but "Hercules" gritted his teeth and bore it stoically. As the grafts mounted, he discovered the special hell that grafting brings. In the healing process grafts shrink so that they become taut, tough, and tight as a drumhead. The painful pull of the shrinking skin is only part of the misery; another part of it is that the shrinkage restricts mobility, making a simple movement an act of torture. Struggling against the cruel straitjacket his grafts were becoming, Hurtubise exercised relentlessly, forcing arms and legs to flex and bend until the skin cracked and bled. When the bleeding stopped he resumed the battle to compel mobility to return to his limbs.

But neither medical skill nor Hurtubise's own unflagging efforts could do anything for his maimed hands. Of all the burns, those on the hands were the worst. The little finger of the left hand, incinerated to the bone, had to be amputated. The tendons controlling movement in the remaining fingers were so damaged that they were no longer functional, leaving both hands drawn up clawlike. The doctors explained that they could operate to rearrange the fingers into another position but that the operation would be irreversible, making the new position permanent. Hurtubise's response was immediate. "Fix my fingers into a curl so that they can be hooked around a steering wheel," he said. That was when the suspicion began to grow that "Hercules," defying all logic, intended to attempt a return to the track.

Nine months and countless operations after his tragic accident, Jim Hurtubise left Brooke Army Hospital. The burn experts, the plastic surgeons, and the therapists had demonstrated that the hospital richly merited its fine reputation, but even medical magic can accomplish just so much. Merely surviving had been no small miracle for Hurtubise. But that was not enough for him. He headed north to Tonawanda in pursuit of an even bigger miracle.

Before leaving Texas, Hurtubise had tried to drive a car. Though his movements had been stiff and slow, he had succeeded. He was certain that the awkwardness would disappear, given time and exercise. The big hurdle would be those hands. The permanent curl the doctors had put into his fingers enabled him to hold a wheel, but the flesh was so sensitive that the slightest pressure on it sent stabs of pain knifing into him. In Tonawanda he went to work on those hands. Some years earlier he had bought a small farm on the edge of town and now he spent hours there driving a truck and a tractor, ignoring the pain in his hands as he forced them against the hard steering wheel while the vehicle jounced over ruts. Gradually protective callouses grew and the pain receded, though it never quite disappeared.

The 1965 racing circuit was now moving into high gear and "Hercules" was resolved to be part of it. He chose the 150-mile Phoenix race for his comeback attempt. USAC officials debated his entry into the contest, doubtful that anyone could endure what he had and still compete on a professional track. In the end they granted consent, not without misgivings.

Buckled into his racing harness, goggles pulled down to the bridge of the nose that doctors had created to replace the one that had been burned away, Hurtubise was tense as he waited for the starting flag at Phoenix. After the flag dropped, after he pushed down on the gas pedal and his engine roared its response, the tenseness left him. He drove skillfully, confidently, taking the turns smoothly and coming down fast into the straightaways. He was heedless of both the hurt in his body and the cheers of the crowd, heedless of everything except the race itself. His hands were puffed and aching at the finish but he had come in fourth. He had proven to the

USAC officials that he belonged back among the pros.

In May, Jim Hurtubise returned to Milwaukee, returned to the track where one year earlier he had been trapped in a flaming pyre. He was everybody's sentimental favorite but most experts gave him little chance of winning; they knew he would not only have to beat his rivals but would also have to overcome the psychological burden of racing at the track that had almost killed him.

From the very start Jim Hurtubise drove as though that one-mile, asphalt oval held no nightmare memories for him. He was again "Hercules," again the charger floorboarding the pedal in a bid for the lead. On the 65th mile he got that lead and held it. It was a long race—250 miles—an exhausting test for any driver. For Hurtubise it was especially exhausting but he maintained his torrid pace mile after mile. He won the race by a wide margin. It was much more than a racing victory. It was a victory for courage and fortitude and the indomitable human spirit.

Index

About the Author

VERNON PIZER is the author of numerous books and of several hundred articles in such magazines as *Saturday Evening Post, Reader's Digest,* and *Esquire.* His work has also appeared in major magazines in Europe and the Far East and has been collected in anthologies. He has covered a wide range of subjects—foreign and military affairs, science, social problems, travel, and personality profiles—but he has always had a lively interest in the people and events of the world of sports, as *Glorious Triumphs* so clearly demonstrates.

After having lived in Washington, Paris, Vienna, and Turkey, Mr. Pizer and his wife, Marguerite, make their home in Georgia where, he says, "good freshwater fishing is only fifteen minutes away from my typewriter."